Iris Murdoch's Comic Vision

Iris Murdoch's Comic Vision

Angela Hague

Selinsgrove: Susquehanna University Press
London and Toronto: Associated University Presses

Associated University Presses
440 Forsgate Drive
Cranbury, NJ 08512

Associated University Presses
25 Sicilian Avenue
London WC1A 2QH, England

Associated University Presses
2133 Royal Windsor Drive
Unit 1
Mississauga, Ontario
Canada L5J 1K5

Library of Congress Cataloging in Publication Data

Hague, Angela.
Iris Murdoch's comic vision.

Bibliography: p.
Includes index.
1. Murdoch, Iris—Criticism and interpretation.
2. Comic, The, in literature. I. Title.
PR6063.U7Z67 1983 823′.914 82-42638
ISBN 0-941664-00-7

Printed in the United States of America

To Judith Jacobson
and Mary Grimes

Contents

Preface

One of the most common adjectives used to describe Iris Murdoch's fiction is *puzzling*. In her book on Murdoch, A. S. Byatt says that the novels at first seem "like puzzles," Walter Allen in a 1971 interview admits to being "still somewhat puzzled" by her work, and Frederick Karl says her achievement as a novelist "remains puzzling."[1] It is significant that these critics also express a sense of uneasiness with the comic dimension of her work. While they and other critics mention the comic tone of her novels as an important aspect of the fiction, few have attempted either to explain or to define the particular nature of her comedy; as Donna Gerstenberger notes, Murdoch's fiction is generally considered within the context of her critical theories, philosophical writings, or use of mythic patterns because of the difficulties involved in analyzing the intention and tone of individual novels.[2]

Murdoch, who has frequently acknowledged her respect for the comic mode, stated in a 1964 interview that she wishes to be considered a comic writer:

> I wouldn't object to being called a comic novelist. On the contrary, I hope that even in the most serious sections of my later novels a strong current of comedy is still to be seen. I don't think one can avoid it in a novel. In a play it is possible to limit one's scope to "pure" tragedy or "pure" comedy, but the novel is almost inevitably an inclusive genre, and breaks out of such limitations. Can one think of any great novel which is without comedy? I can't.[3]

According to Murdoch, the novel must contain comedy if it attempts a realistic portrayal of human life: "If the novel does in some sense hold up a mirror to life, it is bound to have strong elements of comedy, because there is so much which is funny in life: especially if we extend our definition of 'funny' a little to include strange, incongruous, bizarre, ironic. . . ."[4] Iris Murdoch has not been analyzed thoroughly and sympathetically as a comic novelist, and this study is an attempt to provide just such a critical perspective on her fiction. It is my thesis that the comic dimension and ironic tone of Murdoch's work are as important to an understanding of her novels as is her use of mythic patterns and philosophical ideas. In fact, there is a close relationship among these elements, for she often uses archetypal structures for comic effects, and her philosophical writings shed an important light on her critical opinions about the aesthetic and moral validity of comedy as a literary mode.

This study of her comic vision has three parts: (1) a discussion of comic theory and its relationship to fiction; (2) an argument that comedy is an important and positive characteristic of Iris Murdoch's fiction, including a discussion of comic structures, techniques, and tone in her novels; and (3) a detailed analysis and interpretation of three of her most recent novels.

To begin with, chapter 1 summarizes the ideas of the major comic theorists, discusses the implications of their theories for comic fiction, and outlines predominant characteristics of the British comic novel in the twentieth century. Chapter 2 discusses Murdoch's use of comic techniques and tone in relation to her beliefs about comedy and fiction. The remaining three chapters are devoted to a close analysis of the comic structure and tone of three novels that most clearly represent Murdoch's comic and fictional theories in the novel form: *An Accidental Man* (1971), *The Black Prince* (1973), and *The Sea, The Sea* (1978).

In *An Accidental Man*, Murdoch's fictional depiction of the relationship between comedy and contingency, she creates an "accidental" world in which her characters search futilely for pattern and predictability. In *The Black Prince*, the novel that contains Murdoch's clearest statements about irony, she explores the comic possibilities of irony and its potential as a narrative device. *The Sea, The Sea* uses the relationship of art to life, a recurrent concern in her fiction, as its comic premise, and the novel's postscript is a fictional representation of her belief in the final impossibility for art to impose form upon the flux of what she calls "transcendent reality." Each of these novels shows Murdoch at the height of her powers as a comic novelist and substantiates Ronald Bryden's prediction that "with each book she moves forward in mastery, setting herself and encompassing larger goals, advancing steadily toward the great, deep comic classic she is surely going to write within our lifetimes."[5]

It is hoped that this study will supply an enlightening and much-needed comic perspective on this "puzzling" English novelist.

Acknowledgments

The author would like to thank Fred L. Standley for his help and support in the preparation of this manuscript, and Viking Penguin Inc. and Chatto and Windus Ltd. for permission to quote from *An Accidental Man*, *The Black Prince*, and *The Sea, The Sea*.

Iris Murdoch's Comic Vision

1
Introduction

In general, critics tend to be hesitant about defining or describing comic literature, even when their subject is a study of a comic writer or comic elements in an author otherwise considered serious. One reason for this hesitancy is the difficulty in defining what is comic, for even a cursory examination of classical and modern comic theory shows it to be rife with contradictions and diametrically opposed definitions. This discussion will begin with a summary of the ideas of several of the more influential comic theorists, among them Sigmund Freud, Henri Bergson, George Meredith, Susanne Langer, and Northrop Frye, before proceeding to a description of the major characteristics of modern British comic fiction.

Because these theorists deal with various aspects of the comic and present very different interpretations of what constitutes comedy, their ideas are of central importance to a critic undertaking the problematical business of analyzing comic fiction. Freud concentrates on wit in his study, while Bergson sees the comic in mechanized human responses and static situations. For both Bergson and Meredith, comedy is a corrective that combats negative forces in society; Meredith describes comedy as a means to expose and punish egotism and folly. Langer's vitalistic theory, directly opposed to Bergsonian rigidity, defines comedy as a "rhythm of life," a positive, dynamic force. Finally, Northrop Frye's definition of comedy in literature in terms of the comic and ironic modes is an effort to explain the presence of contradictory elements in comedy.

Freud's major contribution to comic theory, *Wit and its Relation to the Unconscious*, deals with wit as one aspect of the comic, "the contribution to the comic from the sphere of the unconscious."[1] Freud sees one of the major functions of wit as triumphing over an "enemy," a release of hostility that in primitive times resulted in physical abuse. More civilized societies translated this hostility into verbal invective[2]; when abusive language became improper, wit evolved as a way to humiliate the enemy through ridicule and laughter. Freud describes wit as having four major functions: obscene wit overcomes our inhibitions of shame and decorum, while certain other types of wit overthrow our critical judgment, shatter our respect for institutions and truths, and attack our belief in rationality. Many jokes go beyond an attack on authoritative persons and institutions and mock the certainty of any kind of knowledge or facts. He agrees with Bergson that automatic, mechanized behavior is comic, and believes that wit depends upon an "absolute psychic agreement" between the person making the witticism and his audience.

Freud states that one of the major characteristics of wit is economy: we laugh at puns and wordplay because they compress meaning, and usually laugh at any kind of excessive expenditure of energy, particularly if it is physical in nature. This principle of economy also operates in humor, but in this instance the pleasure is a result of what he calls "economy of sympathy." The writer or joke-teller takes the emphasis away from the painful aspects of a situation and redirects attention to an area less painful.[3] Humor, then, is an evasion of emotional feeling, a defense mechanism against psychological pain. In his later essay "Humor," Freud defines humor as a rejection of reality, a refusal of the ego to be distressed by the problems that reality presents. Humor is "the triumph of narcissism, the victorious assertion of the ego's invulnerability."[4] Humor, an act of rebellion and a liberating activity that refuses to acknowledge the horrors of reality, can take two forms: a person may adopt a humorous attitude toward others as a means of protection, or may develop this attitude toward himself in order to avoid possible suffering. Although Freud does not explicitly define the major difference between wit and humor as the difference between aggressive and defensive behavior, it appears to be an obvious distinction: wit, in his theoretical scheme, usually involves an attack on others, while humor is a defensive stance. His theory that wit often attacks our belief in rationality while humor is a refusal to accept reality parallels Bergson's belief that comedy involves a relaxation of the rules of reasoning and social conventions. Both theorists note the close relationship between the logic and structure of dreams and jokes, a characteristic discussed later as pertinent to the importance of fantasy in comic literature.

Perhaps the most thorough and influential discussion of comedy, Bergson's essay "Laughter" goes beyond the area indicated by its title. Bergson begins by observing that the comic can exist only in the human realm (animals are laughable only when they exhibit human characteristics), that laughter is always accompanied by an absence of feeling, a "momentary anesthesia of the heart," and that laughter is always a group activity, implying a "secret freemasonry, or even complicity with other laughers."[5] Bergson's major tenet, however, is that all comedy is dependent upon our reaction to what he calls "mechanical inelasticity." The fundamental law of life, according to his theory, is the negation of repetition, a law comedy violates by creating mechanized characters and situations that stress automatic behavior and mechanical repetition. When human beings appear to react mechanically, or attempt to mechanize nature itself, laughter is always the response, just as any depiction of man as a purely physical being is funny.

In the section of his essay on the comic element in situations, Bergson isolates three major comic actions. Because reality itself is never repetitive, recurring incidents or words usually become comic. Comedy often presents an inverted world in which traditional figures of authority are at the mercy of the whims of formerly powerless or socially inferior individuals. The third basic comic situation, what Bergson calls the "reciprocal interference of series," consists of a situation that belongs simultaneously to two independent series of events and can be interpreted as having two different meanings at the same time.

Bergson describes the comic character as one whose outstanding characteristic is his inability to adapt, an inflexibility which leads to the eccentricity that comedy attempts to modify and bring in line with the needs of society.[6] Vain and generally out of touch with the society that surrounds him, the comic hero is rigid and/or unsociable; his flaw, unlike that of the tragic hero, is not moral in nature. Similarly, comic vice differs from tragic vice in that it does not become incorporated into the character and retains an existence independent of the individual, who becomes merely attached to the vice. As a result, the vice itself becomes the central character, and the comic hero, unlike the tragic hero, is simplified rather than complicated by his flaw. The comic character is a type rather than an individual, and a resemblance to a type is always amusing because it shows a human being falling into a ready-made category rather than asserting his individuality and uniqueness. Thus, says Bergson, comedy gives us only general types, and is the only art form that aims at the general.[7] Although the comic hero may be under the erroneous impression he is free to act, in reality he suffers from a lack of freedom, and comedy often reveals this character to be a puppet-figure manipulated by more powerful forces. He lacks the range of choices open to most characters or the self-knowledge of the tragic hero, and he is comic in proportion to his ignorance of himself. Poetry and tragedy analyze the depths of the souls of the characters; comedy is outwardly oriented, deals with direct observation, and its results are always general.

Bergson views comedy as having an "equivocal nature," belonging "neither altogether to art nor altogether to life."[8] In fact, he makes a distinction between comedy and what he calls "genuine art," stating that "comedy lies midway between art and life. . . . it turns its back upon art. . . ."[9] The apparent reason for Bergson's qualification of comedy as an art form is its realism. Tragedy aims for sublimity, which necessitates changes in the "raw materials" the poet utilizes; light comedy and farce are also highly unrealistic forms. "High" comedy (Bergson does not define this term) begins to approximate life itself: "There are scenes in real life so closely bordering on high-class comedy that the stage might adopt them without changing a single word."[10] There seems to be a fundamental contradiction in Bergson's theory of comedy, for he simultaneously states that it is "anti-life" in its use of repetition and rigidity, yet at the same time is the most realistic of the art forms. His belief that comedy presents types rather than individuals is also at variance with his realistic theory of comedy.

George Meredith's contribution to comic theory, "An Essay on Comedy," stresses the intellectual and corrective aspects of the genre. Comedy, which Meredith distinguishes from satire, irony, and humor, "laughs through the mind . . . it might be called the humor of the mind," and its purpose is to "awaken thoughtful laughter."[11] A test of the degree of a country's "civilization" is its comic tradition; the English, according to Meredith, have the proper basis for comedy because they value the common sense that civilization depends upon for its existence. Comedy, which always strives to restore common sense, never takes an antisocial position, for Meredith believes that society is the "wiser world" that comic characters usually contrast with.[12] The purpose of comedy is to attack folly, unreason, and sentimentality, and to temper both optimism and pessimism. Meredith concludes the preface to *The Egoist* by describing the imps that later preside over the birth of Willoughby Patterne, imps that "love to uncover ridiculousness in imposing figures. Wherever they catch sight of Egoism they pitch their camps, they circle and squat, and forthwith trim their lanterns, confident of the ludicrous to come."[13] His novel is a comic treatment of the egotistical Willoughby Patterne and the price he pays for self-centered folly. Like Bergson, Meredith isolates egotism as one of the most important characteristics of the comic hero and would be comfortable with Freud's theory that the evolution of wit parallels the development of civilization. Unlike Freud, however, he views comedy as a means to restore common sense, or rationality, and his theory avoids the irrational, Dionysian elements of the comic.

Susanne Langer's essay on comedy in *Feeling and Form* presents a theory of comedy that underscores its vitalistic and positive aspects. Defining laughter as a "surge of vital feeling," she believes that comedy is the aesthetic form closest to the rhythm of biological reality and as a result is a celebration of fecundity and physical existence. Because good comedy is a reflection of all aspects of biological truth, its all-inclusiveness must depict the more cruel dimensions of life. Langer is among those critics who view comedy from the perspective of Francis Cornford in *The Origin of Attic Comedy*. Cornford's thesis, that comedy is a development of ancient religious rituals that included the *agon* between the *eiron* and *alazon* and culminated in the carrying out of death and the victory of spring/rebirth over winter/death, is the basis for those theorists, including Northrop Frye, who emphasize comedy's mythic and regenerative characteristics.

In keeping with its expression of the "pure sense of life," comedy assumes that after the end of the story comes "more life, more destiny." Unlike the conclusive form of tragedy, comedy is ruled by Fortune rather than Fate and is "essentially contingent, episodic, and ethnic; it expresses the continuous balance of sheer vitality that belongs to society and is exemplified briefly in each individual. . . ."[14] Comedy creates a world in which there is no permanent defeat or human triumph, for the world continues to exist after the incidents of the plot. Tragedy, a closed, final, and passional form dependent upon a sense of individuality, moves toward fulfillment and self-consummation; comedy, on the other hand, expresses the vital rhythm of self-preservation.

Langer's view of the comic hero as a vital, intelligent, and flexible figure differs sharply from Bergson's conception of the typical comic character. She describes him as showing "brainy opportunism in the face of an essentially dreadful universe . . . an image of human vitality holding its own in the world amid the surprises of unplanned coincidence," and characterizes comic action as the "upset and recovery of the protagonist's equilibrium, his contest with the world and his triumph by wit, luck, personal power, or even humorous, or ironical or philosophical acceptance of mischance."[15] The comic character does not change or develop as does the tragic hero, for he is bent on insuring his survival and triumph. In *The Philosophy of Fine Art*, Hegel notes this victorious, positive quality of the comic hero, describing him as one who is in control of his surroundings and is able to remain stable in a shifting, chaotic world. In comedy, says Hegel, "we have a vision of the intrinsically assured stability of the wholly personal soul life"; the general basis of comedy is "a world in which man has made himself, in his conscious activity, complete master of all that passes as the essential content of his knowledge and achievement."[16] Comedy is associated with a self-confidence and geniality that can survive the dissolution of the character's goals and expectations; the comic hero can rise above failure with spontaneous amusement and retain control of himself and his environment as the tragic hero cannot. Here Hegel's conception of comedy differs sharply from that of Freud, who describes the typical comic situation as an individual placed in relation to an "often all-too-powerful outer world."[17] It is obvious, too, that for Langer and Hegel the comic hero is completely different from Bergson's rigid, unsociable hero, and that the vitalistic theory of comedy contradicts the corrective comedy of egotism and ridiculousness that Bergson and Meredith describe.

The above discussions reveal the widely differing theoretical descriptions of comedy. Northrop Frye's theory of modes in *Anatomy of Criticism* is helpful in explaining the various types of comic structures and characters that cause Langer and Bergson to arrive at almost totally contradictory definitions of comedy. Frye, who places comedy midway between the romantic and ironic modes, says that as comedy begins to move toward irony or romance it begins to develop characteristics of these modes. This accounts for the wide range of tone and structure in comedy, which, although its characterization and structural patterns remain fairly constant, can range from savage irony to wish-fulfillment romance. The modes are not necessarily genres, but rather constitute types of structures or moods, what Frye calls narrative pregeneric elements of literature, or *mythoi* or generic plots.[18] The comic mode generally contains a plot structure that places certain obstacles between the hero and heroine, and the comic resolution consists of the victory of the characters over these forces in order that a new society can be created around the united pair. As a result, comedy always aims at social integration and attempts to include as many people as possible at its conclusion; these groups may include undesirable characters, although an expulsion of the *pharmakos* may be necessary. The tragic mode, on the other hand, is comedy's polar opposite and tends to isolate its hero; the comic hero is usually a young man who rebels against the society of the *senex* and is ultimately victorious. Comedy, which depicts a stable and harmonious world that folly temporarily disrupts, creates an upheaval that gives way to a restoration of stability at the conclusion. It is apparent that Frye's plot structure is similar to Cornford's theory of comedy as an *agon* between summer and winter, for Frye says that "this ternary action is, ritually, like a contest between summer and winter in which winter occupies the middle action; psychologically, it is like the removal of a neurosis or blocking point and the restoration of an unbroken current of energy and memory."[9] Because comedy is a movement from an arbitrary, elderly, ritualistic society to one controlled by youth and pragmatic freedom, it is therefore a movement from illusion to reality, and it is easy to see that Frye's regenerative conception of comedy places him in the camp occupied by Cornford, Langer, and Hegel. He goes beyond these theorists, however, by explaining the darker aspects of comedy that have puzzled other theorists in his theory of the ironic mode.[20]

Comedy's tone becomes progressively darker as it moves toward irony, and this kind of comedy often presents a nightmarish world that inflicts pain on a helpless victim or may contain a *pharmakos* figure. The hero often fails to effect any change in his surroundings or chooses simply to flee the situation, which may disintegrate without anything taking its place. The role of the demonic world becomes increasingly important, and the comedy may approach a crisis near the end that is potentially tragic, what Frye calls the "point of ritual death," a crisis that may be a change in tone rather than an actual event. The structure of the ironic mode is a parody of romance that applies romantic mythical forms to works containing more realistic content, a fusion of romantic myth and realism that works in unexpected ways. Satire, which Frye defines as "militant irony," has clear moral norms and standards by which the grotesque and absurd can be measured; invective is satire that contains very little irony. Irony, on the other hand, is evident when the reader is not sure what the author's attitude or his own should be, and it can contain completely realistic content while suppressing the author's attitude. As irony moves from the low mimetic, comic mode of realism and emotionless observation toward myth, mythical structures such as sacrificial rituals and dying gods once again reappear. Clearly, Frye's theory of comedy provides an inclusiveness and flexibility missing in the other theorists. While he is in agreement with Langer's and Cornford's belief in the vitalistic, resurrective nature of comedy, his description of comedy that includes both romantic and ironic elements allows it to venture into the areas of fantasy, fear, demonism, and death, areas their theories exclude. Bergson's rigid, mechanized comic figure becomes, in Frye's scheme, one aspect of the comic situation, the blocking *senex* character who is usually vanquished by the new society created around the victorious comic hero.

Several other recent critics have attempted to integrate the classical theories of comedy and arrive at more expanded definitions. In his essay "The Meanings of Comedy" Wylie Sypher discusses the reasons for the dualistic, ambiguous nature of comedy; Morton Gurewitch in *Comedy: The Irrational Vision* stresses its irrational elements; and in *Tragedy and Comedy* Walter Kerr describes comedy as a pessimistic genre that is a *development* of tragedy rather than its opposite. Another theorist, Robert Heilman in *The Ways of the World: Comedy and*

Society, interprets comedy as an attitude of acceptance and tolerance toward the multiplicity of human existence.[21] Each of these critics discusses important characteristics of comedy that are pertinent to a description of the comic novel.

Like Northrop Frye, Wylie Sypher wishes to explain the presence of certain dark elements in comedy that seem incongruous with its vitalistic, resurrective conclusions. Accepting Cornford's thesis of the ritualistic basis for comedy, he describes the dualistic characteristics of comedy as "both hatred and revel, rebellion and defense, attack and escape."[22] Comedy, he says, is simultaneously revolutionary and conservative, and socially both sympathetic and persecutory. Because comedy is a descendant of the ritual that included both human sacrifice and a feast-celebration of rebirth, it remains essentially an improvisation with a loose structure and specious logic that can include various sorts of improbable events. Sypher believes, as does Joseph Campbell, that tragedy is an incomplete part of the full cycle of drama, encompassing only birth, struggle, and death.[23] Comic action, because it includes the rebirth of the hero, has a wider range of possibilities and is a more expansive aesthetic form that constantly seeks new developments.

The comic hero is a more expansive, flexible individual than the tragic hero, and he can cope with a wider variety of experiences. Sypher disagrees sharply with Bergson's description of the comic hero as a mechanized automaton and speaks of the "resilient vitality" of the comic character. Comedy's basis in conflict and ritual accounts for the presence of pessimistic elements in the comic structure, and as a result it often depicts what Sypher calls the "boundary situation." The boundary situation places the individual at the very edge of rationality and provides a glimpse into chaos and absurdity that negates past values and assumptions; if survived, however, the experience may indeed "save" the individual. Sypher appears to be describing what Frye has termed the "point of ritual death," which often occurs in comedy as it moves toward the ironic mode, and he views comedy as ultimately positive in that it shows the comic hero learning to accept the irreconcilables in man's existence. Though in certain kinds of "conservative" comedy the scapegoat figure must be banished, comedy frequently does not need a victory for its conclusion. Sypher, like Bergson, believes that comedy is a more realistic art form, but thinks that comedy's aesthetic potential is increased because it is a more "pervasive human condition than tragedy," and it "touches experience at more points than tragic action."[24] The comic artist begins by accepting the absurd and improbable and can therefore include incoherent and unpredictable events in his work more freely than the writer of tragedy. It is comedy that admits the disorderly into art, and these disorderly, grotesque elements depend on an "irrational focus." Sypher agrees with Freud that comedy is close to the unconscious, irrational realm, and that there is a close connection between the disjointed, illogical events of both dreams and comedy.

Morton Gurewitch, who uses the irrational basis of comedy for his study of comic theory, acknowledges his debt to Freud and wants a more expanded definition that can include the importance of irrationalism and farce. "Comedy itself is too diverse to subserve a single, exclusive quality or function; that is why it is neither the advocate of Meredithian mind nor the exponent of Plautine release."[25] His basic premise, that comedy is a celebration of irrationalism, stresses comedy's emphasis on illogic, irreverence, disorder, and disinhibition. Gurewitch discriminates between satiric comedy, which "delights in the laughing murder of untenable ideas," and ironic comedy, which treats ideas as mere "colorful or intriguing toys," because he wishes to focus on farcical comedy, a more devastating genre that "promotes a subversion of mind itself by seeking out the powerful pleasures of irrationality."[26] The exhilarating nature of comedy (and more particularly farce) is a result of its defeat of reason in an absurd world, its tendency to celebrate contingency and illogic.

Like Gurewitch, Robert Heilman finds earlier definitions of comedy too limiting. He disagrees with the theory that comedy functions as a corrective, for he believes that the great comic writers are usually generous to humanity and do not rely on a feeling of superiority as a basis for their art. He states that descriptions of comedy as the spirit of the life force, or as the presentations of the disharmonies or discrepancies of human existence, are inadequate. For Heilman, comedy is based on an acceptance of the world and is an affirmative, conciliatory mode "less given to position-taking than to living with different positions as inevitable rather than improvable, as bearable if not always lovable, as amusing rather than contemptible, as expectably imperfect rather than destructive or fatal."[27] Comedy creates a world of rational accommodation in which aggressive drives are tempered by a communal realization that adjustment insures survival: its essence is social and based on coexistence with other people. An anti-Romantic genre that places its faith in group wisdom rather than individual vision, comedy is a "public" art form unlike tragedy, which is enacted in the psyche of the individual. Comedy is the opposite of satire, which is a rejective position, and rather than rejecting the horrors of the world, such as illness and death, it tends to treat them as natural and inevitable.[28] The comic mode attempts to come to terms with complex actuality; rather than excluding or rejecting pain, comedy accepts it as one more fact of life.

Heilman, who agrees with those theorists who note comedy's tendency toward inclusiveness, believes that the comic mode generally tolerates heterogeneity and accepts the fundamental disparity of the world. As a result, comedy's ultimate material is what he terms the "multiplicity theme," often presenting, for example, multiple versions of love. This multiplicity of content creates a multiobjectivity from which we learn to view variety as "equivalence." Heilman echoes Sypher's belief in comedy's expansive nature and wide range: "The multiplicity form is one aesthetic evidence of the impulse to expand the scene, to open it out. . . . The multiplicity form opens the stage to a wide range of characters; it permits the introduction of various eccentrics without falling into a doctrinaire contrast of the deviant and the normal. . . ."[29] Heilman's definition of comedy as a mode that tends to withhold judgment and support social rather than individual well-being is important for several of the comic novelists discussed later, particularly Iris Murdoch.

Walter Kerr discusses comedy as a development or "shadow" of tragedy and interprets it as ultimately pessimistic in outlook. Comedy is a "footnote," or completion of the tragic mode, an aesthetic form that adds the last bit of truth to tragedy's message: the fact that Greek tragedies were followed by the satyr play, which inverted the serious nature of the earlier dramatic action, explains comedy's function as an art form. Kerr states that comedy is not inherently funny, that the best comedy is always harsh. "To be funny is to have been where agony was," he says, and he believes that comedy usually has a forced ending that calls into question the possibility of "happiness and forever after."[30] In fact, comic endings are actually a denial of the true comic spirit and are accomplished only by means of artifice and magic. The comic hero's reaction to the threatening universe is a decision to circumvent it, and as a result he is usually an outsider or vagabond by choice. The comic hero's exceptional ability to evade situations—what Kerr calls "an infinite grace" in going roundabout—"may account for the circuitousness of much comic construction . . . and an improvisational looseness."[31] Comedy circles the action of the narrative while tragedy penetrates its center, just as comedy, unlike tragedy, tends to contain fantasy, because tragedy involves real freedom and free choice; the presence of fantasy, chance, and accident in comedy underscores its tendency to make limited use of free will.

The above discussion of comic theory illustrates the contradictions and ambiguities that confront the critic attempting a definition of comedy, issues that are equally problematical when a description of the comic novel is undertaken. It is obvious that any discussion that includes novels as dissimilar as *Decline and Fall*, *Lucky Jim*, *Murphy*, and *The Black Prince* should concentrate on general tendencies rather than on an arbitrary definition of the genre. What follows is an outline of the major characteristics of the modern British comic novel with an emphasis on the kind of comic world posited, its hero's attributes, and the particular tone that distinguishes comic fiction. Each of the novels discussed does not contain all the events, characters, or tone that are set up as a model for the comic novel. Each does, however, contain a representative group of comic characteristics.

The world presented by the comic novel is generally one of fluidity and inversion, a world in which metamorphosis and sudden dynamic change are the rule. Freud's belief that wit is an attack on man's rational explanations of the universe is pertinent here, for the comic novel is intent on overturning our belief in causality, rationality, and predictability, and reflects man's need to transpose and transform what he normally considers static reality. As Enid Welsford, in *The Fool, His Social and Literary History*, notes, the medieval Feast of Fools and the Christmas Pantomime were real-life events that symbolized society's need to invert social patterns and authority, and man's delight in the possibilities of transformation.[32] The Christmas Pantomime of 1805 in England featured a feigned transformation of the physical world by a clown figure, while the Feast of Fools, like the Roman Saturnalia, was a time of relaxation and reversal of laws, social customs, and ideals. This topsy-turvy world was presided over by a Lord of Misrule and featured a burlesque of the Mass.[33] The comic novel incorporates this theme of reversal and metamorphosis in its treatment of society and the individuals who make it up.

The society presented in comic fiction is often an inverted one in which persons in positions of authority and power reveal themselves to be incompetent and/or corrupt. Earlier dramatic comedy often featured pedants, quack doctors, and shyster lawyers; the modern British comic novel often focuses on academics and the world of academe. Tom Sharpe's *Porterhouse Blue* contains the largest assortment of academic fools, but the teacher-as-buffoon or hypocrite also occurs in Evelyn Waugh's *Decline and Fall*, Malcolm Bradbury's *The History Man* and *Stepping Westward*, David Lodge's *Changing Places*, and Kingsley Amis's *Lucky Jim*. In modern comic fiction the need to overturn and burlesque symbols of authority and dignity represented in earlier comedy by the church or medical profession is replaced by satirical portraits of school and university life, ruled by incompetent and sometimes sinister teachers. In this sense, academe functions as a kind of microcosm of society, and its breakdown is a reflection of the dissolution of a rational, predictable, ordered world. As the aptly named Dr. Fagan, the shady headmaster of Llanabba Castle in *Decline and Fall*, remarks, "I have been in the scholastic profession long enough to know that nobody enters it unless he has some very good reason which he is anxious to conceal."[34] In *Hurry on Down* Charles Lumley revisits his former school in an attempt to humiliate schoolmaster Mr. Scodd and his "shambling regiment of pedagogues" in a scene that combines adult hostility with adolescent wishfulfillment fantasies.[35] The portrayal of Welch in *Lucky Jim* and Jim Dixon's Merrie England speech are a direct attack on academic life and values, and Dixon's self-acknowledged hazy knowledge of his subject is equaled only by his lack of interest in it; in *Porterhouse Blue* Tom Sharpe subjects Cambridge to the same scathing irreverence that Amis uses in his depiction of provincial university life. The comic novel attempts to invert more than academe, however. *Decline and Fall's* drunken surgeons, peasantlike aristocrats, and millionaire butlers inhabit a world in which all values and expectations are overturned, just as Charles Lumley attempts to create a new life for himself by radically altering his environment, trying to live in a working-class world diametrically opposed to his middle-class upbringing. Iris Murdoch usually transforms the lives of her characters by allowing them revelations that alter their previous conceptions of themselves and others, realizations of the past or present that are usually sexual in nature and create different angles of vision for the people involved.

The comedy of this topsy-turvy world frequently has a diabolical tone. The relationship between comedy and the darker, demonic aspects of life has already been explored in Northrop Frye's theory of the relationship between comedy and irony. Enid Welsford indirectly touches on this in her description of the Feast of Fools, a celebration that often featured bringing into church an ass that punctuated the Mass with brays and howls; although Welsford does not compare these happenings to the Sabbat of devil worshipers, which includes the use of animals, the chanting backwards of the Mass, and the desecration and inversion of the religious ritual, the correspondences between the two seem clear, and they underscore comedy's affinity with satanism. Welsford does, however, mention that the comical figure of Harlequin has his origin in a much more demonic character; she notes that a variant spelling of his name is Hellequin and that he "appears first in history or legend as an aerial spectre or demon, leading that ghostly nocturnal cortège known as the Wild Hunt."[36] Ronald Wallace observes that evil is a powerful force in most comedy and that modern comic fiction contains "a dark force or power loose in the universe, a vague, undefinable, intractable thing that pervades modern life and takes shape in the individual."[37] Evelyn Waugh's novels contain a great deal of this "vague, undefinable, intractable thing," for some dark force seems determined to torture Tony Last in *A Handful of Dust* and Paul Pennyfeather in *Decline and Fall*. In Muriel Spark's *Memento Mori* much of the comedy results from the reactions of the aged characters to the telephone calls announcing the inevitability of their deaths by an unknown, demonic voice that is never rationally explained in the book; in the same way Dougal Douglas's satanic characteristics enable him to manipulate the people and events in *The Ballad of Peckham Rye*. Iris Murdoch is perhaps the greatest practitioner of this kind of demonic comedy, fusing comic and satanic elements in her novels in a way that disorients some readers.

Metamorphosis and fluidity are as important to the comic novel as its tendency to invert traditional patterns and expectations. The dynamic, shifting world of this type of fiction reflects both the expansive, irrational nature of a great deal of comedy and its refusal to accept the strictures of complete realism, or what Harold Watts describes as the linear, inevitable progression of tragedy.[38] As a result, the comic novel usually stresses movement, action, and vitality. Charles Lumley describes the spirit of his comic world in a way that emphasizes its energy and power:

> Whatever the outcome, he belonged to the world where real actions were undertaken. He belonged with Froulish thumping his typewriter in a derelict loft, Dogson getting himself murdered in the quest for a story, even with Ern serving a prison sentence or Mr. Blearney getting up dreary leg-shows in the provinces. The people he belonged with were ill, disgusting, unsuccessful, comic, but still alive, still generating some kind of human force. . . . As ever, the serious point had emerged through the machinery of the ludicrous. His life was a dialogue, full of deep and tragic truths, expressed in hoarse shouts by red-nosed music-hall comics.[39]

Charles Lumley, like many comic heroes, views his life as capable of personal transformation, and comic novels frequently reveal the transformational potential of both character and situation. Though comedy is sometimes criticized for failing to show proper development of character or reasons for radical changes in the personalities of its characters, these transformations are an integral part of comedy's structure, which emphasizes human adaptability and potential for metamorphosis. Sudden dramatic changes in characters tend to be comic because they call into question our conception of human nature as essentially static, just as comedy attacks our belief in a causally connected, predictable universe. Evelyn Waugh allows his characters to metamorphose suddenly into radically different personalities in *Decline and Fall* in order to create a comic world in which human nature is capable of endless transformation. Enid Welsford describes "the source of comic delight" as "the pleasing delusion that facts are more flexible than they appear to be," and Waugh extends this principle to the human personality, creating characters that shock and please the reader in their flexibility and fluidity.[40] In the course of *Decline and Fall* Dr. Fagan regularly changes professions, Philbrick creates various identities and pasts in order to survive, and Grimes stages phony deaths so that he can be reborn into new and less dangerous identities. Kingsley Amis's heroes, who use disguises, practical jokes, and role-playing for manipulative purposes, are capable of assuming almost any persona in order to extricate themselves from trouble and to exploit the situations they find themselves in. Iris Murdoch's characters, frequently overtaken by sudden, unpredictable onslaughts of romantic love, are transformed suddenly into foolish, undignified monomaniacs. Nigel Dennis's *Cards of Identity*, which uses the fluid, ephemeral nature of human identity as its premise, best exemplifies this characteristic of comic fiction.

In general, this conception of the comic character as both changeable and flexible is, as Langer has noted, positive and reflects the ability of the comic hero to survive events that would destroy a less resilient individual. Harold Watts believes that the progression of tragedy is linear and moves inevitably toward death, while comedy's structure is cyclical, circular, and regenerative. Bergson touched on the circular nature of comedy in "Laughter" in his statement that life always moves forward and does not repeat itself, and he mentions that circularity and repetition are therefore comic (and unrealistic) themes. Though not all comic novels conclude with the hero's return to his initial situation or have him experience a series of repetitive events, the circular nature of comedy and its relation to the theme of survival is an important one. In *Decline and Fall* Paul Pennyfeather, after undergoing expulsion, imprisonment, and a falsified death, ends up where he began, studying theology at Oxford. Garnett Bowen and John Lewis are in almost exactly the same situation at the conclusion of *I Like it Here* and *That Uncertain Feeling* as they were in the beginning, and Wain's *Hurry on Down* ends with Charles and Veronica reunited.

Comedy's cyclical structure can be interpreted as lacking narrative and character development and as implying a world view that sees progression as impossible; however, a circular narrative insures the survival of the hero and the creation of the "world of safety" that Watts describes as necessary for a comic vision of the world, frequently bringing about the "restoration of stability" that Frye discusses. Initially there appears to be a contradiction between the cyclical plot structure of some comedy and the world of constant change it posits, for although the comic character may metamorphose frequently, he often returns to his original situation. In general, however, the comic hero retains a basic core of stability of character (Hegel says that this stability is an important characteristic of the comic hero) while he continues to adapt to the shifting world about him. Thus the circular and ultimately safe, stable world of comedy results from the comic character's ability to transform himself at will.

The survival of the comic hero is related to his flexible nature, and this quality makes him capable of successful actions in the world of change and inversion that comedy presents. Though there are exceptions to this (Murphy and Bradley Pearson in *The Black Prince* die, while Tony Last in *A Handful of Dust* meets a worse fate, forced to read Dickens to a madman in the jungle for the rest of his life), in general the comic hero is a survivor who depends upon his wits and adaptability to emerge unscathed from the terrible events that occur around him. In this sense the comic hero and the picaresque hero have much in common, and among their similar characteristics are a talent for survival and the "protean nature" that insures it.[41] Wylie Sypher describes the comic hero as characterized by an ability to change identities, calling him the "archetypal hero of many guises" who "wears motley—the parti-color of human nature—and quickly changes one mask for another, putting on indifferently and recklessly the shifting features of man, playing with gusto more roles than are suitable to the tragic hero."[42] Amis's Jim Dixon, Garnett Bowen, and John Lewis all share a gift for lying fluently, play-acting, and assuming disguises. Like Spark's Dougal Douglas, Charles Lumley makes a career out of a series of assumed identities and jobs and proves he is a comic survivor even more overtly when he recovers from a potentially fatal automobile accident, in the process eluding the police and his band of smugglers. Many of the characters in *Decline and Fall* reveal their abilities to survive catastrophic events, even in the face of a supposed death, but it is Grimes who emerges as the archetypal comic hero when he both stages his own "deaths" and then proceeds to "resurrect" himself. Upon hearing that Grimes is finally dead, Paul Pennyfeather knows better:

> Paul knew that Grimes was not dead. Lord Tangent was dead; Mr. Prendergast was dead; the time would even come for Paul Pennyfeather; but Grimes, Paul at last realized, was of the immortals. He was a life force. Sentenced to death in Flanders, he popped up in Wales; drowned in Wales, he emerged in South America; engulfed in the dark mystery of Egdon Mire, he would rise again somewhere at sometime, shaking from his limbs the musty integuments of the tomb.[43]

Waugh's "life force" is a literary representation of Langer's description of the comic hero. An important figure in comic literature, Grimes is clearly a descendant of Falstaff, another character who knows that a feigned death can insure survival. The comic hero's immortality, a reflection of his vitalistic, dynamic world, is dependent on his skill in playing various roles, at times even impersonating death itself. The indestructibility of the comic hero reveals him to be quite close to the comic figure described by Cornford and Langer, and illustrates comic art's emphasis upon continuity and immortality. Iris Murdoch's *An Unofficial Rose* begins with a death but is otherwise devoted to the concept of survival: "People survive," the narrator observes repeatedly, and the fact that life usually does go on for a majority of people underscores the comic potential in human experience. In fact, "people survive" is a central tenet of many comic novels.

The comic hero's expertise in assumed identities and disguises has another important ramification for comic fiction: the close relationship between the comic hero and the artist-figure.[44] The comic character is an individual who enjoys manipulating people and events; he takes an unabashed interest in the life going on around him and often wishes to go a step beyond passive enjoyment, consciously creating new situations that are usually humorous. Even if he is not an artist in the traditional sense, he may begin to view himself as a kind of artist-figure, constructing new events in the plot of his own life and manipulating the fates of those around him; the dissembling and practical jokes present in so many comic novels are, for the comic character, acts that are almost akin to the creation of a work of art. Stuart Miller, in *The Picaresque Novel*, calls this principle the "art theme" and believes it to be an important element of picaresque fiction. The picaro, in order to survive in the chaotic, menacing world around him, must become a trickster. He soon moves, however, from using tricks as a means to an end to gratuitous trickery; the trick becomes an artistic activity for the picaro, an indication of his attempts to "conquer reality."[45] Wain's Charles Lumley and Amis's heroes play elaborate practical jokes on others, usually both as a means of revenge but also for pure enjoyment; they become, in a sense, surrogates and reflections of the narrator himself, arranging and orchestrating the people around them. The "power figures" in Iris Murdoch's fiction attempt more elaborate and destructive ways of creating new realities: characters such as Julius Irving in *A Fairly Honourable Defeat* and Effingham Cooper in *The Unicorn* treat life as art with tragic results.

The comic writer often takes this characteristic of the comic hero one step farther, creating a protagonist who is an actual artist. Iris Murdoch's fiction is filled with both failed and successful writers, and the majority of these characters play the role of buffoon. In Joyce Cary's *The Horse's Mouth* Gulley Jimson views the world simultaneously as a comic drama and as fodder for his art; his treatment of the physical world, particularly the Beeder's apartment, merely as raw material for artistic creation is an attitude that is in itself comic. Amis's Garnett Bowen is a dissatisfied writer who combines a comic and hostile world view; and in *Hurry on Down*, John Wain's depiction of Froulish, the would-be Joycean novelist, is another example of the writer-as-buffoon. The comic novelist often depicts the writer as a fool, a practice that curiously calls into question the validity of artistic activity, or the comic writer will use an artist as narrator or major character in order to have a consciousness capable of the sensitivity and detachment necessary for the narrative. Detachment, usually an important characteristic of the comic hero/narrator, enables him to recognize the inverted world of comic discrepancies and contradictions. An example is Jim Dixon's satirical description of the article he is attempting to publish so that he can keep his job, an attitude possible only because of his own emotional distance. Martin Lynch-Gibbon in *A Severed Head* is another extremely detached observer of his own problems. After learning that his wife is having an affair and planning to divorce him he goes home and sleeps soundly, remarking, "How well one sleeps when one is in grief."[46] In *Hurry on Down*, despite Charles's statement that he prefers involvement with the people around him, he is detached enough from his own life to reduce its incidents to a one-paragraph comic allegory, complete with capital letters.

The presence of fantasy in comic fiction is related to the comic hero's vision of life as art and his tendency to be an artist in many novels. Beckett's description of the "first zone" of Murphy's mind is an excellent paradigm for the fantasy consciousnesses of many comic characters. Just as the practical jokes and tricks of the picaro and comic hero show their need for revenge *and* aesthetic activity, Murphy's fantasy zone accomplishes both creation and retaliation. The zone contains:

> the elements of physical experience available for a new arrangement. Here the pleasure was reprisal, the pleasure of reversing the physical experience. Here the kick the physical Murphy received, the mental Murphy gave. It was the same kick, but corrected as to direction. Here the chandlers were available for slow depilation, Miss Carridge for rape by Ticklepenny, and so on. Here the whole physical fiasco became a howling success.[47]

Murphy's first zone, like the comic world, is inverted, fluid, and creative, a zone in which Murphy can be in control of events rather than at their mercy. If the comic hero cannot manipulate his world in reality, he will accomplish it in fantasy, and this tendency to treat life as art allies him closely to the artist-figure. Freud's definition of humor as a rejection of the horrors of reality is applicable to comic fantasy, and his belief that wit is a function of the unconscious is also relevant to comic fantasy, which often utilizes the irrational elements present in dream states. The comic writer may regard the fantasy experience as necessary, comic, and creative, as does Kingsley Amis, or as comic and destructive, as does Iris Murdoch, but in each case the comic hero's need to fantasize reflects his desire to expand and create new versions of reality and is an important feature of his dynamic, inventive personality.

One of the most important characteristics of comic fiction is the particular attitude it adopts to deal with narrated events. In "Notes Toward a Comic Fiction" Robert Bernard Martin states that this comic tone creates a world of "safety" dependent upon the psychical distance of the narrator, a style that insures that no ultimate catastrophe will come to the characters. He observes that quite often even the opening sentences of comic novels alert the reader to the fact that he has entered a world in which a "compact of safety" is implied between writer and reader. The comic novel depends upon an air of artificiality, which results in the psychical distance that is its most important characteristic. Martin believes that the very presence of the narrator can increase the sense of invulnerability in comic fiction and uses Thackeray's authorial preface in *Vanity Fair* as an example. Certainly the presence of an omniscient narrator can create this sense of safety, but, as Wallace notes in his discussion of the comic novel, first person narration is also an effective comic technique which allows the narrator simultaneously to expose himself unconsciously as foolish and to assure the reader, by the fact of the existence of the novel, that he has lived to tell the tale.[48]

Martin correctly identifies a feeling of inviolability as an important characteristic of comic fiction and isolates narrative technique and artificiality of diction as the means by which this sense of security is communicated. Other means, however, are available to the comic novelist who wishes to distance the reader from the novel. Wallace discusses the fact that much comic writing has what he calls a "discontinuity of form and content" and notes that the modern comic novelist frequently makes use of a refined, even lyrical style to express violent and absurd events: "The ironic incongruity between language and action comically reflects the larger incongruities which structure the plot."[49] The writer may use a discrepancy between content and form to create comic effects and to distance the reader from the events that are being narrated.

Wallace also mentions the tendency and potential of modern comic fiction to parody other fictional forms, particularly the picaresque novel and the romance comedy. Beckett goes beyond parodying any particular type of fiction in *Murphy* and instead parodies the novel form itself; the narrator reduces character description to a list, addresses the reader as "gentle skimmer," and in general parodies many of the techniques of representational fiction. Picaresque characteristics are obviously an important aspect of such modern novels as *The Horse's Mouth*, *Hurry on Down*, and *Under the Net;* Iris Murdoch, Kingsley Amis, and John Wain use the traditional plot structure of the lovers separated by evil forces as part of their narrative structure. Murdoch uses this device more ironically, however, in novels such as *The Black Prince* and *An Accidental Man* than does Amis or Wain. Wallace does not discuss the relationship between parody and the distance that comedy is dependent upon for many of its effects. Parody, a particularly comic form because it imposes a greater distance between the novel itself and the reality it is attempting to recreate, constantly forces the reader to acknowledge the fact that the work he is reading is based upon the existence and conventions of another literary genre. Rather than being content with reflecting and expressing the reality of the content of the novel, the parodic novel expects to be interpreted in light of the literary form being parodied. Like comedy, parody is a less realistic and more self-conscious art form.

Even if the comic novel is not parodying another narrative structure, it often exhibits a self-conscious and self-reflective quality that undercuts realism of content. The comic novel will often call attention to itself as a made object; *Murphy*, David Lodge's *How Far Can You Go?*, and several of Iris Murdoch's novels are examples. Murdoch's writer-narrators worry, as in *The Black Prince*, about where the most artistically effective point is to begin the novel, or, like Charles Arrowby in *The Sea, The Sea*, anguish over what genre is the most appropriate form for the work. In *How Far Can You Go?* Lodge's narrator (who at the conclusion of the novel introduces himself as Lodge) admits there are limitations to his omniscience, refers to an earlier novel written by the author, and frequently breaks into the narrative in order to destroy the fictive illusion. The comic novel often attempts to shatter its own imaginary reality, a tendency that makes it a more self-conscious genre that appears to value the artistic achievement as more important than the reality it reflects. Just as the comic hero sees life in aesthetic terms and attempts to function as an artist in his manipulation of people and events, the comic novel treats the art form as of ultimate importance, often sacrificing realistic representation for artifice and unreality. The comic hero's attempt to control his environment through disguise, trickery, and fantasy is paralleled by the comic artist's tight and sometimes intrusive control of narrative structure and use of artificial language. Comedy would appear to be an intrinsically more artificial art form that celebrates the art-for-art's sake philosophy, despite the fact that it frequently uses realistic content and a loose, episodic plot structure. If tragedy, as some critics define it, is the genre that presents man as ultimately conquered by forces greater that himself and beyond his control, comedy can be seen as the artist's attempt to take control of his art form and in turn allow his hero to manipulate his own fate, thereby insuring his survival and victory over the forces that surround him. Harold Watts's theory that man has created cyclic myths that are the basis for the comic world view so that he can feel "in calm imaginative control" of his life is important for the comic novel, where both the narrator and comic hero exemplify this need for an imaginative command of the world.[50] Hegel's description of the comic hero as the "complete master of all that passes" is an accurate one for many of the comic heroes of modern British fiction.

2

Iris Murdoch's Comic Fiction: Theory and Practice

There is little disagreement among critics that Iris Murdoch's fiction contains comic elements that are an important aspect of her work. Problems arise, however, in critical evaluations of her use of comedy, for although several critics praise what is usually described as her "wit," others believe that the humorous tone of her novels, coupled with the serious and sometimes tragic nature of the subject matter, creates an unresolved tension that undermines her achievement as a novelist. The following discussion will look briefly at the critical reaction to Murdoch as a comic writer and will analyze her opinions about comedy and their relation to fiction; comic techniques in her novels will also be surveyed and evaluated.

Frederick Karl is among those critics who are uneasy about the combination of tragedy and comedy in Murdoch's novels. In *A Reader's Guide to the Contemporary English Novel* he makes a severe attack on her use of comedy, stating that she is unable to sustain her humorous talents for more than a scene or interchange between characters, a failure that causes her novels to become more and more trivial. Although he admits that Murdoch is expert at social comedy and witty dialogue, he denies that this has improved her fiction and accuses her of creating what he calls a kind of "puppet show" that reflects the "somewhat sadistic need on the author's part to see people perform for the pleasure of others."[1] Karl believes that Murdoch is unable to synthesize the serious and witty aspects of her fiction, a view shared by June Sturrock, who states that *The Black Prince* is flawed by its comic tone: "the over-activity of her comic gifts . . . flourish[es] often to the disadvantage of the novel as a whole."[2] Larry Jean Rockefeller, who also takes a negative view of Murdoch's comic talents, criticizes her for not creating the novel of character she has frequently praised in her critical writings: like several other critics, Rockefeller has an unfortunate tendency to judge Murdoch's novels by her critical essays, particularly "Against Dryness," and this study of comedy in the early novels is hampered by both this approach and the premise that satirical comedy is inimical to character creation. Rockefeller is almost unreservedly antagonistic to the comic elements in Murdoch's fiction, calling them inhumane and intolerant and maintaining that her satiric attitude toward her characters actually functions to "dehumanize" them.[3]

Such negative opinions, however, are in the minority. Although most Murdoch critics tend to deemphasize the comic dimension of her work, preferring, as Donna Gerstenberger has noted, to search for mythic patterns or to evaluate her fiction in terms of her critical and philosophical writings, for the most part critics agree that she is a successful and accomplished comic writer. The fusion of comedy and tragedy that distresses Karl or Sturrock is praised by others as one of Murdoch's greatest strengths as a novelist. Frank Baldanza, who admits that he has difficulty specifying the exact nature of her comedy, nonetheless believes that the "main thrust of her genius is toward the comic vision" and compliments the "rich array of examples of various comic modes—comedy of manners, comedy of character, knockabout farce, and intellectual wit" that she employs in such a way that no one mode predominates over the others.[4] In her book on Iris Murdoch, A. S. Byatt rarely discusses the comic dimension of her work, but does note her "rather wry, rather dry wit,"[5] while William Van O'Connor praises her "fine sense of fantasy and comedy" and believes that "many of her more fascinating characters are comic grotesques."[6] Several critics who greatly admire Murdoch as a novelist comment on her successful union of comedy and tragedy, and an understanding of this characteristic of her fiction is essential to an understanding of Murdoch's comic vision. In his excellent study of the early fiction, *The Disciplined Heart: Iris Murdoch and Her Novels*, Peter Wolfe concentrates on a philosophical interpretation but does mention that her work is in the tradition of the social comedy of the British nineteenth-century novel. However, says Wolfe, Victorian social comedy did not contain the tragic depth present in Murdoch's fiction, and he praises her boldness and originality in fusing the two genres: "What incites pity and terror in her novels is the recognition that, without a supervening preserver, the line between comedy and tragedy becomes less fixed and less arbitrary." [7] William Hall, Donna Gerstenberger, and G. S. Fraser also note Murdoch's talent for blending the serious and comic.[8] Murdoch's statements about comedy and tragedy in her philosophical writings, interviews, and novels provide valuable insights for the critic attempting to understand the puzzling synthesis of comic and tragic elements in her fiction, for Iris Murdoch has made both an aesthetic and philosophical defense of comedy and its importance for the novel.

Fiction, she believes, is the genre best suited for realistic and comic presentations of life; theater and poetry, on the other hand, are the proper domains of tragedy. In an early essay, "The Sublime and the Good," she says that the inability of the novel to portray tragedy is a failure: "The novel fails to be tragic because, in almost every case, it succumbs to one of the two great enemies of Love, convention and neurosis."[9] However, her attitudes about the relative importance of comedy and tragedy and their relation to fiction have undergone a gradual change in her career as a novelist. She now believes that comedy is as intrinsically important and truthful as tragedy, and as such is a proper vehicle for the novel; in fact, she now maintains that comedy, the most realistic mode, is best suited for fiction, in her opinion the most realistic of the arts. Murdoch's increasing faith in the aesthetic validity of comedy has been evident in her most recent fiction; deeply committed to comedy as the most appropriate and realistic form for the novel, she has increasingly allowed the comic mode to dominate the work of the past decade.

In a 1968 interview with W. K. Rose, Murdoch conceded that tragedy is a superior art form, but based her belief that the novel is a comic genre on the fact that fiction does not have the limitations inherent in tragedy: ". . . I think the novel is a comic form. I think tragedy is a highly specialised and separate form. Doubtless it's the highest of all art forms, but it depends on certain limitations which a novel can't have. The novel is always comic."[10] As does Henry James, Murdoch believes that the novel has limitless potential and is the most nonrestrictive of the literary genres. "I think it's a great big form. The only restrictions are my restrictions, or my limitations. I feel like somebody who's living in a great big house and just occupies a tiny corner of it."[11] This "lack of limitation" is closely related to the novel's realism. She has expressed her desire to be a realist, to write novels that contain a much simpler type of realism, which includes presentations of "ordinary life and what things are like and people are like and so on, and to create characters who are real, free characters."[12] Murdoch perceives a close relationship, also, between reality and comedy, and believes that because life itself is comic the novel best fulfills its potential when presenting the absurd, contingent, and comic dimensions of reality. In a 1978 interview she says that life is not what she calls "dramatic" because it lacks the "shape" that drama imposes; life is "comic and absurd. It may be terrible, but it is absurd and shapeless. . . ."[13] She emphasizes this idea in another interview, reiterating that the novel is a comic form and that its comic potential is a positive quality that results from fiction's all-inclusive, nonrestrictive nature. Tragedy is not an appropriate model for the novel because "almost everything is comic. I think tragedy is a very small form which belongs to poetry and theatre. Of course, some of the greatest works of literature are tragedies but are not, as such, models for the novel. However sad and awful the things it narrates, the novel belongs to an open world, a world of absurdity and loose ends and ignorance."[14]

Murdoch's characters frequently voice her own philosophical tenets, and her recent fiction contains, not surprisingly, characters who echo her belief in the fundamental absurdity of the human predicament. Montague Small in *The Sacred and Profane Love Machine*, for example, instructs Blaise Gavender not to "play" his life so tragically. Life, he says, "is absurd and mostly comic. Where comedy fails, what we have is misery, not tragedy."[15] In *A Word Child* Hilary Burde laments that his life lacks the grandeur and potential for tragedy: "It all remained, for me, grossly muddled up, penitence, remorse, resentment, violence, and hate. And it was not a tragedy. I had not even the consolation of that way of picturing the matter. Tragedy belongs in art. Life has no tragedies."[16] Charles Arrowby, the retired theatrical director of *The Sea, The Sea*, echoes Hilary's statement that only art can do justice to tragedy: "Thus life is comic, but though it may be terrible it is not tragic: tragedy belongs to the cunning of the stage."[17] The "cunning" of the theater is its artifice and tight structure; the novel, with its close relationship to what Murdoch calls the "contingent, messy" world, is the best vehicle for comedy and the realism upon which comedy is based.

Murdoch has clearly made an aesthetic defense of comedy as the most realistic vehicle for fiction. However, because she is also a moral philosopher whose literary criticism and fiction often reveal her ethical beliefs, she has also attempted a philosophical argument in favor of comedy. Her study of Plato, *The Fire and the Sun: Why Plato Banished the Artists*, is in the main an attempt to explain the philosopher's distrust of art, particularly its tendency to present false pictures of reality and to distance us, through indirectness and irony, from reality. In the process she makes her own defense of art based on Plato's objections, justifying the ludicrous and absurd against his censure and discussing the moral validity of a comic world view. Murdoch defends the absurd against Plato's objections that it is degrading and is instead receptive to the Zen concept of the *koan*. Plato, she says, "contrasts with his Zen colleagues who . . . take the funny as central to the human pilgrimage. The *koan* appears as some sort of wild joke. Of course, there is a bad absurd (degrading, hurtful), but is there not also a good absurd? Loss of dignity need not be loss of moral stature, can be surrender of vanity, discovery of humility; and a sense of the ludicrous is a defence against pretensions, not least in art."[18] Plato, says Murdoch, equates the dignity of the individual with virtue, an equation she cannot accept. She instead believes that it is necessary to ask if it is possible to be truly humble with unimpaired dignity and comes close to stating that being perceived as ludicrous, or viewing oneself as ludicrous, is necessary for the attainment of humility that increases our potential for goodness. In *Henry and Cato* the priest Brendan Craddock expresses this idea more clearly, telling Cato that an ignorance of our own absurdity actually creates evil:

> "Our chief illusion is our conception of ourselves, of our importance which must not be violated, our dignity which must not be mocked. All our resentment flows from this illusion, all our desire to do violence, to avenge insults, to assert ourselves. We are all mocked, Christ was mocked, nothing can be more important than that. We are absurdities, comic characters in the drama of life, and this is true even if we die in a concentration camp, even if we die on the Cross."[19]

She later calls the "good absurd," which can help act as a protection against pretension and egotism, the "sublime absurd," which can be either comic or tragic. This sense of the sublime absurd is actually an understanding of the "structural problems of the Demiurge . . . insight into where the 'faults' come."[20] Good art, she maintains, is art that presents a revelation of reality and often makes use of the absurd; as a result, good art often has a certain playful quality that in no way negates the seriousness of the revelation. She says that "art is playful, but its play is serious . . . the playfulness of good art . . . delightedly seeks and reveals the real."[21] In his postscript to *The Black Prince*, P. Loxias talks about the playful nature of art and the absurdity of humanity. "Art is to do with joy and play and the absurd. Mrs. Baffin says that Bradley was a figure of fun. All human beings are figures of fun. Art celebrates this."[22] For Murdoch, the playful tone of art, a characteristic of her own fiction for which she has been criticized, is a deliberate philosophical, moral, and aesthetic stance; art, and specifically the novel, presents us with the ludicrous aspects of human life and reveals the "faults" both of the Demiurge and of human nature. The novel's playful tone is the aesthetic correlative of its subject matter, the sublime absurdity of the human condition.

Murdoch believes that seeing reality unencumbered by personal fantasy or romanticism is a moral necessity; art, she says, "can enlarge the sensibility of its consumer" and provides "clear realistic vision with compassion." Because the ultimate reality is death, it is "the role of tragedy, and also of comedy, and of painting, to show us suffering without a thrill and death without a consolation."[23] In light of her statements about the moral dimensions of comedy, it is logical that she thinks that artists need to depict human mortality comically, to portray not "fake prettified death" but what she calls "real" death: "The only thing which is of real importance is the ability to see it all clearly and respond to it justly which is inseparable from virtue. Perhaps one of the greatest achievements of all is to join this sense of absolute mortality not to the tragic but to the comic."[24] Comedy, the most realistic of the literary vehicles, is the proper mode in which to present the most important reality, death. Murdoch believes that comedy is the proper aesthetic mode for the novel and is a philosophical and moral necessity for art; and her fiction reflects her conviction that the most horrible aspects of existence can be dealt with effectively and truthfully in the comic mode.

One of the main tendencies of comic fiction, as discussed earlier, is its attack on the conception of a rationally ordered world. Iris Murdoch shares this lack of faith in man's ratiocinative, logical nature, and her novels, which often use the failure of rationality as a basis for their comedy, reflect her belief that art should include the accidental, contingent dimensions of reality. The contingent functions as a reminder that human will and planning are often helpless before the random, jumbled events that elude the human desire for rationality, causality, and order. In her essays Murdoch emphasizes the fundamental disorder of human consciousness, and in "The Idea of Perfection" she says that it is necessary for us to accept "a darker, less fully conscious, less steadily rational image of the dynamics of human personality."[25] She is of the opinion that existential freedom of choice is too optimistic a philosophy, that human nature is more complex, less rational and free, than the existentalists maintain:

> The existentialist picture of choice, whether it be surrealist or rational, seems unrealistic, over-optimistic, romantic, because it ignores what appears to be a sort of continuous background with a life of its own; and it is surely in the tissue of that life that the secrets of good and evil are to be found. Here neither the inspiring ideas of freedom, sincerity, and fiats of will, nor the plain wholesome concept of a rational discernment of duty, seem complex enough to do justice to what we really are. What we really are seems much like an obscure system of energy out of which choices and visible acts of will emerge at intervals in ways which are often unclear and often dependent on the condition of the system in between the moments of choice.[26]

Although quick to point out that she does not consider herself a Freudian, Murdoch nevertheless agrees with Freud's "realistic and detailed picture of the fallen man," what she calls his "thoroughly pessimistic view of human nature." Freud's description of human nature, one that stresses man's lack of rational control, is closer to her own:

> What seems to me . . . true and important in Freudian theory is as follows. Freud . . . sees the psyche as an egocentric system of quasi-mechanical energy, largely determined by its own individual history, whose natural attachments are sexual, ambiguous, and hard for the subject to understand or control. Introspection reveals only the deep tissue of ambivalent motive, and fantasy is a stronger force than reason. Objectivity and unselfishness are not natural to human beings.[27]

Her statement in "Against Dryness" that we "are not isolated free choosers, monarchs of all we survey, but benighted creatures sunk in a reality whose nature we are constantly tempted to deform by fantasy" summarizes her conception of the human condition, and her fiction uses this generally pessimistic view of man as irrational and at the mercy of forces beyond his control for comic purposes.[28] In *Sartre, Romantic Rationalist* she commends the novelist's ability to portray human reason as limited: the novelist describes rather than explains and understands "that human reason is not a single unitary gadget the nature of which could be discovered once for all. . . . [The novelist] has as a natural gift that blessed freedom from rationalism which the academic thinker achieves, if at all, by a precarious discipline."[29] According to Murdoch, the novel, the best vehicle for the depiction of the realistic and comic world, is also best equipped to describe man's irrational, contingent existence. Sexual attraction, the inability of human beings to furnish rational explanations and predictions for their behavior, and the contingent, random nature of the universe all create a topsy-turvy world of comic unpredictability in her novels.

It is significant that Murdoch brings up the subject of sex in her discussion of Freud's theory of human personality, for the wide variety of sexual attachments in her fiction is one of the major characteristics of her comic vision. She would agree with Walter Kerr that sex is funny because it is a reminder of man's lack of free choice. No man is free to choose whether or not he is a sexual being, says Kerr, for the entire basis of sex is irrational; sex is an appetite that "cannot be satisfied within reason because reason was not consulted when the appetite was being formed. . . . Man is by nature a planner, and here is nature making an ardent anarchist of him."[30] Murdoch has said that sex is fundamentally what she calls "jumble," and that art can properly deal with sex because it "accepts and celebrates jumble, and the bafflement of the mind by the world."[31] Sex, according to Murdoch, "is a very great mystifier, it's a very great dark force. It makes us do all kinds of things we don't understand and very often don't want to do."[32] Much of the sexual comedy of Murdoch's novels is based on the failed attempts of her characters to rationalize and intellectualize their sexual feelings, to attempt to exert a false control over events and emotions that are in reality manipulating them. Bergson's theory that a staple of comedy is the individual who believes he is speaking and acting freely but in reality is a puppet-figure controlled by others is relevant here, for Murdoch's characters are both controlled by other people and by their own ungovernable emotions. *An Unofficial Rose* stresses the difficulty of the individual's ever knowing if his choices are his own, and characters frequently make decisions that in actuality are a result of the manipulations of other people, although they remain ignorant of this fact.[33]

Many of Murdoch's novels depict persons who attempt to rationalize love and sex. In *A Severed Head* Martin Lynch-Gibbon observes that he is being "coaxed along to accept an unpleasant truth in a civilized and rational way," and Palmer Anderson's repeated statement that "we are civilized people" is indicative of his attempt to place in a false rational focus events such as adultery, incest, and suicide, and by doing so control people and situations. Similarly, in *Henry and Cato* Henry Marshalson's affair with the married Bella Fischer takes place with her husband's knowledge and, it would appear, approval; the narrator ironically notes that both Bella and Russell discussed the situation with their analyst. In *A Fairly Honourable Defeat* Rupert Foster and Morgan Browne believe that the other has become precipitately infatuated; in reality, both are the puppets of Julius Irving. They, like many other Murdoch characters, attempt to rationalize their predicament and repeatedly emphasize the need to "keep their heads." The conversations between Rupert and Morgan are among the most comic scenes in Murdoch's work, a comedy based, as in *A Severed Head*, on man's mistaken faith in his ability to master his emotions and to remain free of the consequences of his irrational acts. In *The Sacred and Profane Love Machine* Harriet Gavender is treated less humorously than Morgan Browne or Martin Lynch-Gibbon, but she too attempts to accept the unacceptable—her husband's infidelity and the presence of his illegitimate son—and by doing so to exercise rational control over the people and events around her. The cocktail-party scene in the novel is reminiscent of the social comedy of *A Severed Head* in which characters gather in a doomed attempt to come to terms with their own passions and sins against each other. Like Honor Klein, Edgar Demarnay functions as the voice of truth and responsibility that expresses the impossibility of politely rational accommodation.

Murdoch's suspicions about the validity of psychoanalysis and her ironic portrayals of psychologists become understandable in this context, for psychotherapy optimistically assumes that explanations for human behavior are possible and that the free will of the individual can effect meaningful changes in the psyche. Marjorie Ryan has noted that Murdoch's humor is often based on "the complicated attempts of the characters to simplify complex human relationships according to their own wishes and in their usually false estimates of themselves and of the situations they are in, despite their continued attempts at analysis."[34] Murdoch's flawed and often sinister psychoanalysts, who include Palmer Anderson, Francis Marloe, and Blaise Gavender, suffer from the delusion that this simplification of complex reality is possible and desirable. These characters can also be indicted for sacrificing the importance of the unique, particularized individual to a general theory of human personality. Palmer Anderson is a powerful figure in the first half of *A Severed Head* but plays a role of decreasing importance, losing both Antonia and Honor, while Francis Marloe remains a buffoon throughout *The Black Prince*. Almost all of Blaise Gavender's patients make comically rendered and near-magical recoveries after his series of misfortunes; one disenchanted patient says of Blaise: "I feel so much better since that ghastly creep passed out of my life. How I wish those dogs had eaten him up!"[35]

The inverted, topsy-turvy world that comic fiction often presents, in which traditional values and expectations no longer hold true, forms the background for many of Murdoch's novels. She usually begins with a presentation of a rationally ordered, socially conventional environment that rapidly gives way to a series of comically unexpected events.

Frank Baldanza says that a typical novel will open with "all the accepted realistic conventions of character, setting and plot" and will then make use of "highly unlikely elements within this context to force to erupt within a set scene something outrageous, quirky, fantastic—so that the reader finds himself embroiled in a particularly unique situation that is wildly far removed from the premises on which the work set out."[36] Many of the novels contain a direct reference to the beginning of a "new world" that shatters the peace and predictability of the past. Before his discovery of his wife's affair with Palmer Anderson, Martin Lynch-Gibbon speaks of the "very last moment of peace, the end of the old innocent world," and Charles Arrowby hopes that regaining Hartley will result in "the old early innocent world" of their childhood "reassembling" around them. Hilary Burde talks about "the last day of the old world," and Rupert Foster, after receiving Morgan's love letter, correctly surmises that "things can never be quite the same again. Our quiet world, our *happy* world, has been disturbed. Life will be anxious, uncomfortable, unpredictable."[37]

This "new world" is often partially brought about by a character from the past reentering the scene, such as Gunnar Jopling in *A Word Child*, Morgan and Julius in *A Fairly Honourable Defeat*, Hartley Fitch in *The Sea, The Sea*, and Hugo and Anna in *Under the Net*. A revelation about the present or past may also destroy prior interpretations and beliefs. Martin's series of revelations in *A Severed Head*, Harriet's discovery of her husband's infidelity in *The Sacred and Profane Love Machine*, and Jake Donoghue's realization that Anna is in love with Hugo in *Under the Net* fall into this category. Characters often lament the destruction of the past by their new knowledge. Hilda Foster's betrayal by her sister radically alters her conception of their past close relationship; her belief that Morgan is having an affair with her husband "injected its venomous power into the whole of her past, changing all that was good into rotten specious appearance. Everything was different now right back to the start."[38] Martin Lynch-Gibbon's new knowledge that his brother Alexander has been sleeping with his wife throughout their marriage has the same effect: "It was as if Alexander had done something to the whole of my past, to years which stretched far back, beyond my marriage, into the nursery, into the womb."[39] A belief in a causally ordered universe assumes that man is capable of a correct interpretation of the past, an ability that Murdoch's characters desire but are often denied with both tragic and comic results.

The new world created by a revelation about the past is usually one ruled by accident and contingency, a universe from which causality and predictability have departed. Murdoch has repeatedly stated her desire to bring jumbled, contingent elements into her fictive world, and her novels are filled with characters who behave unpredictably, eccentric, bizarre individuals who fulfill her wish to write the novel that is a "house fit for free characters." The earlier discussion of comic theory established that comedy is the most appropriate mode for the presentation of an expanding, all-inclusive, contingent world, and Murdoch's novels frequently make use of the relationship between comedy and contingency. William Hall, in his discussion of *The Sandcastle*, believes that the unpredictability of Murdoch's contingent world is responsible for the comic energy of her fiction. P. W. Thomson, who also notes the lack of causal relationships in Murdoch's fiction, thinks that this is a deliberate stratagem on her part.[40] In Murdoch's universe any and all human relationships are possible, and the consequences of these relationships are equally unpredictable. Nigel Boase's letter to Danby in *Bruno's Dream* clearly states Murdoch's belief in the infinite possibilities of human interaction; his declaration that "it is a weird thought that anyone is *permitted* to love anyone and in any way he pleases. Nothing in nature forbids it. A cat may look at a king, the worthless can love the good, the good the worthless, the worthless the worthless, and the good the good"[41] is echoed in Charles Arrowby's remark that "anyone can love anyone." As a result, Murdoch's fiction contains aging and elderly men such as Hugh Peronett, Bradley Pearson, and Charles Arrowby, who behave like foolish, lovesick teenagers, and preternaturally mature adolescents such as Miranda Peronett and Patrick Tisbourne.

The reactions of characters to situations and other people, particularly when familial relationships are involved, are comically unpredictable in Murdoch's novels. Parent-child relationships are often treated humorously; although, as in the instance of the Polish Lusiewicz brothers in *The Flight from the Enchanter*, who treat their mother with less than old-world reverence, the humor may sometimes be rather black:

> "She decay inside," said Stefan. "All is decay. I cannot explain. You smell it soon."
>
> "One day we burn her up," said Jan. "If we insure her we burn her up long time ago. She so dry now, like straw, she burn in a moment. One big flame and all gone."
>
> "We burn you, yes, you old woman, we put fires in your hair!" Stefan would shout, and the old mother would smile again and her eyes would begin to glow feverishly as she looked up at her tall sons.[42]

Morgan Browne states that one of her husband's qualities that she finds particularly unnerving is his relationship with his father: "It's so unnatural for a man to love his father."[43] Similarly, Montague Small in *The Sacred and Profane Love Machine* meditates on the joy his mother felt over his wife's death. "Leonie could not, and indeed scarcely tried to, conceal her satisfaction, but at least she kept away. She had been discreetly 'ill' on the day of the funeral. Perhaps she might have been unable to restrain herself from dancing."[44] Hilary Burde's reaction in *A Word Child* to the news of his Aunt Bill's death is comparable. ". . . I had intended to go out and celebrate but found myself simply sitting at home shedding tears of joy."[45] Given Murdoch's penchant for depicting bizarre family relationships, it is not surprising that *The Italian Girl* contains a scene in which a drunken Otto Narraway collapses with laughter at his mother's funeral:

> I thought for a moment that he was ill or overcome by tears: but then I saw that he was laughing. Monstrous giggles shivered his

> great figure from head to foot and turned, as he tried to stifle them, into wet, sputtering gurgles. "Oh God!" said Otto audibly. He choked. Then abandoning all attempt at concealment, he went off into a fit of Gargantuan mirth. Tears of laughter wetted his red cheeks. He laughed. He roared. The chapel echoed with it. Our communion with Lydia was at an end.[46]

A recurring theme in Murdoch's fiction is the enjoyment people experience because of the misfortunes of others. In *A Severed Head* Martin Lynch-Gibbon observes his sister's difficulty in concealing her glee over his marriage break-up, while in *An Accidental Man* Murdoch extends this characteristic of human nature to the majority of the characters in the novel, at times even allowing individuals to acknowledge the pleasure they take in the catastrophes and deaths of those around them.

It is important to realize that Murdoch does not want the reader to view persons behaving in this fashion as necessarily callous or evil; rather, she is attempting to widen her reader's tolerance for these characters and to show people reacting in ways which, though they may initially appear to be unusual, are actually quite common. Murdoch's desire to create the novel of independent, complex, "opaque" characters results in presentations of individuals who react in unpredictable ways, and these extremely eccentric characters include Mrs. Wingfield in *The Flight from the Enchanter*, Auntie in *Bruno's Dream*, and Leonard Browne in *A Fairly Honourable Defeat*. In *The Lunatic Giant in the Drawing Room* James Hall mistakenly states that Murdoch is not able to sympathize deeply with eccentricity. In fact, in an interview Murdoch has praised Dickens's talent for eccentric characterization: "To come back to . . . eccentricity: Dickens is accused of exaggeration and so on, but I don't think he exaggerates; he just discerns how strange human beings are. This is something which very much belongs to the novel—to emphasize truths which are normally concealed."[47] In "The Sublime and the Beautiful Revisited" she discusses how great novels have a "display of tolerance" for the right of others to a separate mode of existence, and the depiction of eccentric and unpredictable people in her novels is a result of this belief. Robert Heilman's theory that the multiplicity theme is a major characteristic of comedy certainly holds true for Murdoch's fiction, for the reader is asked to accept the strangeness of her characters, and, in many cases, to withhold judgment and dismiss preconceptions and prejudices. The gently comic treatment of homosexuality in her novels, in particular the Theo-Pierce and Ducane-Fivey relationships in *The Nice and the Good* and the sympathetic and detailed description of the relationship between Axel and Simon in *A Fairly Honourable Defeat*, illustrates this. Though these relationships are dealt with ironically to a degree, the reader is unable to categorize these individuals simply as homosexuals or latent homosexuals. In fact, in *A Fairly Honourable Defeat* Murdoch moves beyond the comic stereotype of the effeminately homosexual interior decorator in her portrayal of Simon Foster. Although he remains a comic character throughout the novel (and Murdoch cannot resist the gratuitous comedy of Simon's desperate attempts to dispose of a pink Teddy bear all over London), his personality is more complex than the stereotype upon which it is based, and he emerges as a fully realized, sympathetic, complicated character. The strange romantic pairings in the novels, which frequently involve either great age differences or the presence of incestuous or complex familial relationships, are further examples of Murdoch's attempts to force the reader into an acceptance of a wider framework for human actions.

Northrop Frye has noted that ironic comedy is close to the demonic world and may contain a nightmarish quality generally not considered comical. Much of Murdoch's fiction falls into this category, and a recurring character in her novels is what she calls the "power character," the person who plays the role of a "demon" in the lives of others; in the early novels these characters are rarely treated in a comic fashion. Mischa Fox, Gerald Scottow, Emma Sands, Carel Fisher, and Julius Irving, who commit the chief Murdochian sin of attempting to manipulate the lives of those around them, are not comic characters. (Honor Klein, though a powerful force in *A Severed*

Head, is an exception to this in that she does not try to control the actions of other people.) However, in the later novels, in keeping with Murdoch's increasing vision of the world as comic, these characters become less frightening and begin to be treated humorously. Palmer Anderson is an early example of this tendency, for after being struck by Martin his power is severely curtailed. Bradley Pearson claims that he and Arnold Baffin are both "demonic men," but this is obviously meant ironically, and Hilary Burde fails to function as a power figure toward the end of *A Word Child;* his sister finally eludes his control by marrying, and Lady Kitty dies. The culmination of this tendency to reduce the power figures to comic absurdity occurs in *The Sea, The Sea*, in which Charles Arrowby, the self-acknowledged "magician" of the novel, loses Hartley, Titus, and James, and in the final section of the novel reveals himself as a rambling, elderly man, stripped of influence and importance.

The fact that several critics find the fusion of comic and tragic elements a major flaw in Murdoch's work was mentioned earlier, and any discussion of Iris Murdoch as a comic writer must take into account the suicides and deaths that occur with such frequency in the novels. A frequent tragic motif is the individual who, because he does not receive proper attention, attempts or commits suicide. Although various theorists, among them Walter Kerr, Susanne Langer, and Robert Heilman, have mentioned the presence of cruelty, suffering, and death in comedy, Northrop Frye's theory of the function of the *pharmakos* figure best explains why Murdoch's novels, often otherwise comic in tone and structure, frequently contain the death of at least one character: "Comedy often includes a scapegoat ritual of expulsion which gets rid of some irreconcilable character, but exposure and disgrace make for pathos, or even tragedy."[48] The "irreconcilable" characters in Murdoch's fiction begin appearing in *The Flight from the Enchanter* and continue until *The Sea, The Sea*. The first of these individuals, Nina the dressmaker in *The Flight from the Enchanter*, dies needlessly, and other victims include Georgie Hands, Rupert Foster, Harriet Gavender, Lady Kitty Jopling, Dorina Gibson Grey, James Arrowby, and Titus Fitch. For one reason or another, and the reason is not necessarily a flaw in the character himself, these persons are unable to cope with the events unfolding around them and choose suicide, or may instead be the victims of an "accidental" death that appears fated in the context of the novel. The scapegoat dimension of Dorina Gibson Grey's death in *An Accidental Man* is clearly connoted in Mavis Argyll's comment to Matthew Gibson Grey that Dorina "somehow died for us, for you and me, taking herself away, clearing herself away, so that our world should be easier and simpler."[49] Although the other novels do not voice this sentiment quite so explicitly, it is obvious that these characters often function to take on the sufferings of those around them and to pay a kind of penance for the sins of others. Murdoch's interest in Até, the transference of suffering and pain from one individual to another, is most evident in Max Lejour's discussion of the concept at length in *The Unicorn* and in his conclusion that "it is in the good that Até is finally quenched, when it encounters a pure being who only suffers and does not atttempt to pass the suffering on."[50] Though not all the characters who meet death are innocent victims who pay for the sins of others, the deaths of several of these individuals, particularly Dorina Gibson Grey, Harriet Gavender, and Titus Fitch, have an almost sacrificial dimension.

The presence of death in Murdoch fiction increases its unpredictable quality and extends the range of her comedy, adding a realism often lacking in other types of comic fiction. The "compact of safety" that Robert Bernard Martin discusses as an important characteristic of comedy is conspicuously missing in her fictive world, for the *pharmakos* figures temper the comedy and represent an attempt to fuse the comic and tragic modes. These deaths often correspond to the "point of ritual death" that Frye mentions; several characters who do not die undergo the near death and revelation that Frye and Sypher discuss as a frequent occurrence in comedy. Effingham Cooper in *The Unicorn*, John Ducane in *The Nice and the Good*, Hilary Burde in *A Word Child*, Colette Forbes in *Henry and*

Cato, and Charles Arrowby in *The Sea, The Sea* each survive a close brush with death and are altered in varying degrees by the experience. Murdoch is too much of a realist to allow her characters the extreme metamorphoses of personality that characters in other types of comic fiction often undergo, though Madge in *Under the Net*, Lisa in *Bruno's Dream*, and Constance Pinn and Harriet Gavender in *The Sacred and Profane Love Machine* experience changes in personality and physical appearance that are treated comically.

Although death is a frequent event in Murdoch's world, the theme of survival runs throughout her work and is an important structuring principle for her comedy. Interested in both the physical and emotional ability of human beings to survive, she frequently stresses the transitory nature of emotion. The fact that in reality few people die from love or sorrow is treated humorously in her novels, and she recognizes that this characteristic enables most people to endure tragic and unpredictable events. As a result of their self-protective egos, Kate Gray and Jessica Bird in *The Nice and the Good* make amusing recoveries from their love affairs with John Ducane, just as Blaise Gavender and Edgar Demarnay in *The Sacred and Profane Love Machine* overcome death and disappointment by immediately beginning to think about themselves. Other characters, such as Dora Greenfield and Toby Gashe in *The Bell*, Julian Baffin in *The Black Prince*, Simon Foster in *A Fairly Honourable Defeat*, and Annette Cockeyne in *The Flight from the Enchanter*, survive because of their youthful resilience. However, even Murdoch's older characters have a marked ability to recover from sorrow. Edmund Narraway in *The Italian Girl* observes that most human beings are "brief mourners," and his opinion that bereavement is usually a fleeting emotion is echoed by Mavis Argyll in *An Accidental Man*. The recurring ironic comment in *An Unofficial Rose* that "people survive" reaches its culmination in the last section of *The Sea, The Sea*, appropriately entitled "Life Goes On": after two deaths and the loss of his childhood love, Charles Arrowby escapes a near death to remain as egotistical and deluded as he was earlier in the novel, when he retired to the sea to "repent of egoism."

Physical survival and ephemeral emotion are treated with tolerant comedy in the novels because they are as "real" as death and suffering.

One of the more destructive characteristics of Murdoch's characters is their tendency to view life as art, an attitude mentioned earlier as a frequent theme in comic fiction. In Murdoch's novels, however, while an aesthetic view of life may create a degree of comedy, it often has devastating effects on the lives of individuals. Murdoch, who believes there should be a sharp delineation between life and art, creates characters who regard themselves as actors in a drama or attempt to manipulate others for aesthetic ends, in the process endangering both themselves and others. Madge's theatrical plea to Jake to script *Nous Les Vainquers* in *Under the Net* and Annette Cockeyne's unsuccessful dramatic suicide attempt in *The Flight from the Enchanter* are comical treatments of the human desire to give life a fabricated aesthetic quality, a tendency several characters in *The Unicorn* and Julius Irving in *A Fairly Honourable Defeat* carry to tragic lengths. The people around Hannah Crean-Smith view her as both an aesthetic and religious symbol and, as a result, are unable to prevent her tragic end. Julius Irving sets into motion a series of events that bring about the death of Rupert Foster because Julius, in reality a biochemist, believes he is an artist who creates works of art by orchestrating the lives of those around him; he tells Tallis Browne that the tricks he has played on the characters are a "result of my instinct as an artist." In a less scheming and far less demonic way Mischa Fox in *The Flight from the Enchanter* gives parties that are "as often as not carefully constructed machines for the forcing of various plots and dramas," and his actions indirectly result in Nina's death. Murdoch will frequently emphasize the human tendency to see oneself as an actor in a drama by describing characters as actors or by having characters perceive the reality around them in terms of the stage, a technique she uses to structure *The Sea, The Sea.* In a desire to exert power over others and to view themselves as artist-figures, several of her characters actually claim to have "invented" other people. In *An Unofficial*

Rose Emma Sands claims that she has invented the love affair between Randall Peronett and Lindsay Rimmer, Julius Irving tells Hilda Foster that he has "invented it all," and Garth Gibson Grey admits to Gracie Tisbourne in *An Accidental Man* that he wishes to feel as if he has just "invented" her. Murdoch's philosophical belief in the intrinsic value of the unique individual makes this kind of aesthetic lust for power over real people a serious moral error, and, in another instance of Murdoch's allowing her characters to become spokesmen for her own moral philosophy, Marian Taylor in *The Unicorn* decides that "no one should be a prisoner of other people's thoughts, no one's destiny should be an object of fascination to others, no one's destiny should be open to inspection. . . ."[51] Obviously, there is a close relationship between Murdoch's power figures and the characters who view life as art. Murdoch's distrust of fantasy is related to this theme, for she perceives a distinct difference between fantasy and the imagination; fantasy, she believes, is a distorting, destructive force that can lead to tragedy and that always prevents a clear vision of reality.[52] The true artist utilizes his imagination, an act that results in a work of art that does not entail the manipulation of real people.

Many of Murdoch's characters go beyond regarding life as art and attempt to become actual artists. The number of authors and would-be authors in the novels, too lengthy to list, includes Jake Donaghue, Randall Peronett, Martin Lynch-Gibbon, Marcus and Carel Fisher, Miles Greensleave, Garth Gibson Grey, Bradley Pearson, Hilary Burde, and Charles Arrowby. Quite often the work of art produced by these writers, as in the instance of *Under the Net*, *The Black Prince*, *A Severed Head*, *A Word Child*, and *The Sea, The Sea*, is the novel itself, and these novels, especially *The Black Prince* and *The Sea, The Sea*, have a self-reflexive nature that is a result of first person narration by the novelist. However, Murdoch does not allow the self-conscious quality of the narrative to lessen in any way its realistic content, and in fact the narrator's self-consciousness and the self-reflexive structure of the books actually serve to intensify their realism. The creation and existence of *The Black Prince* and *The Sea, The Sea* are an integral element of the plot, for, while Murdoch may distrust treating life as art, she wants the reader to perceive the art work as a direct product of the experiences of her main characters. Because she does not seek the air of complete artificiality found in comic novels such as *Murphy* and *Decline and Fall* but instead attempts the creation of a realistic fictive world, she avoids direct parody, choosing instead to make occasional use of mythic or generic structures. In an article on literary allusions in her early novels, Howard German notes that "her novels seldom display an *extended* parallel with an earlier work . . . her practice is perhaps closer to that of Eliot in *The Waste Land* than to that of Joyce in *Ulysses*."[53] Murdoch is more intent on creating a particularized, unique world for the reader than on parodying past conventions, and the comedy in her novels results from human interaction and actual happenings rather than parodic comparisons with other novels or literary structures. Both Bradley Pearson and Charles Arrowby are concerned about the form and structure of their own books, sometimes using them as vehicles for espousing their aesthetic theories. First person narration, as Ronald Wallace has observed, is an inherently comic device that provides the comic assurance that the main character has survived to tell the story (a convention that Murdoch cleverly deviates from in *The Black Prince*) and allows the narrator to reveal himself either as a liar attempting to deceive the reader or as simply deluded by circumstances. Murdoch is adept at exploring all the comic possibilities of first person narration, and many of her finest novels take this form.[54]

Murdoch's first person narrators are often comic characters who inadvertently reveal their own egotism and obsessive fantasies to the reader. Hilary Burde in *A Word Child* allows his self-hatred and fear of other people to negate the comic possibilities that the early portion of the novel contains; the tone of the novel changes from the wry self-deprecation of the beginning to an almost vitriolic hostility by its end. Murdoch seems unsure about what the tone of this novel should be and loses sympathy with her narrator during the course of the narrative, problems which do not occur in her treatment of Jake Donaghue, Martin Lynch-Gibbon, Bradley Pearson, or Charles Arrowby. The comic tone of these characters' narratives is partially based upon their continual sense of ironic detachment from the events narrated, a detachment that Hilary Burde has lost by the end of *A Word Child.* The production of a novel such as *The Black Prince* or *A Severed Head* is an attempt by the writer/narrator to control his surroundings in the imaginative realm; Barney Drumm's Memoir in *The Red and the Green* is a more obvious example of the artist's talent for using words to create a false picture of reality, to manipulate, both imaginatively and aesthetically, the people around him. Barney realizes that he is using his Memoir to take his wife "captive in the imagination and belittle her, and correspondingly to enlarge himself. He was the wise, detached, shrewd observer, ironical and invulnerable."[55] Barney's description of himself is true of all of Murdoch's first person narrators, and as a result their attempts to maintain a pose of wisdom, detachment, and invulnerability create much of the comic tone of these novels. However much she may allow these characters to appear foolish and reveal their weaknesses to the reader, they are not presented so negatively as some of the power figures who manipulate people in real life; her artist-figures are at least involved in the creation of actual works of art.

Murdoch's belief that written and spoken language is essentially ironic is important to an understanding of the comic dimension of her novels. There appears to be a fundamental contradiction in her view of language, for in "Salvation by Words" she makes a strong defense for the importance of words as expressions of reality:

> Words constitute the ultimate texture and stuff of our moral being, since they are the most refined and delicate and detailed, as well as the most universally used and understood, of the symbolisms whereby we express ourselves into existence. . . . The *fundamental* distinctions can only be made in words. Words are spirit.[56]

In her fiction, however, Murdoch is intrigued with the potential of language to lie, to distort reality, and to create false pictures and situations that are often comical. This view of language is present in *Under the Net* in Hugo Belfounder's statement that "the whole language is a machine for making falsehoods" and is a recurrent theme throughout her fiction.[57] In a recent novel, *The Sea, The Sea*, Charles Arrowby rejoices in the fact that he could write "all sorts of fantastic nonsense" about his life and would probably be believed because of the power of human credulity and the written word. Murdoch frequently presents sections of epistolary narration in the novels and will have her characters draft multiple (and comical) versions of the same letter, more often than not lying and distorting the truth through their manipulation of language. Some of these letters are among the most comic passages in her novels, particularly when the reader is aware that the characters are lying outrageously. In *The Sacred and Profane Love Machine* Montague Small advises Blaise Gavender to reveal his affair with another woman to his wife by letter, because in that way he will be able to present the situation in the most favorable light. The letter, when finally written, is filled with outright lies and false presentations of his past and present relationship with Emily McHugh. Murdoch also allows her characters to reveal their weaknesses and obsessions in their letters. In several instances her letter-writers are peripheral characters whose letters create new comic perspectives: Nicky Cockeyne in *The Flight from the Enchanter* and Patrick Tisbourne in *An Accidental Man* are comic characters who exist, for the reader, only in the form of their extremely amusing letters. *An Accidental Man* carries Murdoch's propensity for epistolary narration to an extreme, for entire chapters consist solely of letters and notes written by one character to another.

Murdoch's most comprehensive statement about the relationship between language and irony and its significance for fiction occurs in *The Black Prince* in one of Bradley Pearson's asides to P. Loxias. Discussing the need of some artists to simplify reality in their art, Bradley says:

Of course, as you have so often pointed out, we may attempt to

> attain truth through irony. (An angel might make of this a concise definition of the limits of human understanding.) Almost any tale of our doings is comic. We are bottomlessly comic to each other. Even the most adored and beloved person is comic to his lover. The novel is a comic form. Language is a comic form, and makes jokes in its sleep. God, if He existed, would laugh at his creation. Yet it is also the case that life is horrible, without metaphysical sense, wrecked by chance, pain and the close prospect of death. Out of this is born irony, our dangerous and necessary tool. . . . How can one describe a human being "justly"? How can one describe oneself? . . . Yet what can one do but try to lodge one's vision somehow inside this layered stuff of ironic sensibility, which, if I were a fictitious character, would be that much deeper and denser? . . . So art becomes not communication but mystification.[58]

Bradley, who *is* a fictitious character, clearly expresses Murdoch's belief that life and art that attempts a realistic presentation are comic. The very nature of language causes it to distort the reality it seeks to express and to become itself an ironic mode of expression. Even the most realistic literary art form, the novel, is essentially ambiguous and ironic because it is made up of words, abstractions that distance the reader from the objects and concepts they name. Though the goal of the novel, for Murdoch, is as close a rendering of reality as is possible, the material it must use to create this reality is inherently laden with ironic, ambiguous, and comic properties. Murdoch uses this characteristic of language for comic purposes in letters, which present multiple versions of reality; in her novels narrated in first person, characters often use language to defend themselves and to distort reality. She also uses the comic possibilities of dialogue in her novels, particularly those of the past decade. Her fiction has become increasingly dramatic in the sense that she frequently eschews authorial comment and simply presents extended conversations between characters, allowing the reader to infer whatever ironic discrepancies may be present. In *The Fire and the Sun: Why Plato Banished the Artists* she observes that though Plato distrusted the entire concept of art he was himself a great artist, for his use of the dialogue form is an aesthetic achievement. "The dialogue form itself is artful and indirect and abounds in ironical and playful devices."[59] Murdoch successfully explores the comic and ironic potential of dialogue, and her later novels contain an increasing emphasis on extended comic-dramatic scenes. Her interest in the theater resulted in the appearance of *The Three Arrows* and *The Servants and the Snow* in 1973 and *Art and Eros* in 1980, plays which, unlike *A Severed Head* and *The Italian Girl*, were written exclusively for the theater, and her concern with dramatic presentation has been used successfully and comically in her more recent fiction.

Though in general Murdoch uses comedy to include the contingent, the unique, and the formless, she also makes use of comedy as a corrective, creating satirical portraits of egotistical persons who suffer from the solipsistic condition that usually accompanies self-obsession. She believes that one of the great human failings is egotism, that solipsism and fantasy are destructive forces that prevent the individual from perceiving reality. Good art can function to extricate the ego-centered person from the distorted, narrow vision of self-interest and can give him an awareness of the world outside himself. In *The Bell* Dora Greenfield learns that art, in this instance a painting by Gainsborough, can rescue her from her solipsistic fantasies:

> Here was something which her consciousness could not wretchedly devour, and by making it part of her fantasy make it worthless . . . the pictures were something real outside herself, which spoke to her kindly and yet in sovereign tones, something superior and good whose presence destroyed the dreary trance-like solipsism of her earlier mood. When the world had seemed to be subjective it had seemed to be without interest or value. But now there was something else in it after all.[60]

Art is a way out of "trance-like solipsism," and Murdoch often creates comical portraits of egotistical men and women who must learn to recognize and accept the importance of the world outside themselves. A typical pattern in the fiction is, as already discussed, the destruction of peace and order and the establishment of an unpredictable new world that is frequently comic: the characters whose peace is disturbed usually must learn that they are not the center of the universe but rather a quite small and sometimes insignificant part of it.

It is not only the individual who is guilty of solipsistic smugness; Murdoch's novels contain several married couples, among them Kate and Octavian Gray, George and Clara Tisbourne, and Rupert and Hilda Foster, whose happiness and self-satisfaction have isolated them from other people and given them a false sense of security and invulnerability. As a result they are treated comically and the events of the plot often function to destroy their complacency. Although Murdoch believes that fiction should always aim for the creation of the unique, particularized individual, this individual can achieve happiness only when he sees his own importance in the perspective of the needs and rights of those around him. Heilman's belief that comedy is an anti-Romantic mode is based on the fact that the Romantics placed their faith in the private personality and wisdom of the individual and that comedy, on the other hand, stresses common sense and communal adjustment. Murdoch has admitted her distrust of the Romantic belief in the ultimate importance of the individual, and though she has a limited faith in his potential for "common sense," the comic vision in her novels corresponds to Heilman's opinion that comedy attempts to emphasize the importance of the group over the single member. According to Heilman, true comedy is not satirical; rather, it works toward an acceptance of a flawed world, which he describes as:

> the over-all medley of the casual, the heedless, the inconsistent, the inexplicable (the uneven distribution of talent and luck), the fallible, the illusive, and even the scheming—a mixed actuality which somehow evades first principles, not really to defy or defend them, but to forget them or limit their applicability, and thus exhibits whole, impure, humanity in action.[61]

Murdoch's comic fiction attempts this presentation of "whole, impure humanity in action"; her comedy is generally one of acceptance and tolerance of contingency, human frailty, and eccentricity. She wants to create a realistic world that can do justice to the ludicrous, incomplete, and accidental "jumble" of everyday life, and by doing so, to express the density and importance of what she has called "transcendent reality." The comic dimension of this presentation of reality is heightened by the fact that the novelist must use words that distort the reality he is expressing. For Murdoch, then, the novel is comic both in its range of content and in the ironic quality of language itself; it now remains to look closely at three novels that best illustrate Iris Murdoch's talent as a comic writer.

3
The Comedy of Contingency in *An Accidental Man*

Iris Murdoch's desire to write realistic fiction that allows her characters to remain free of the author's tendency to impose pattern and form is a recurrent topic in her statements about her own novels. In an interview with Frank Kermode she discusses the temptation of the novelist to "give in to form," or what she calls "myth," to allow the pattern of the novel to draw the characters "into a sort of spiral, or into a kind of form which ultimately is the form of one's own mind."[1] This is not to say, however, that Murdoch is opposed to the presence of form in her fiction; in a later interview she has said that "I think myself that pattern in a novel is very important. . . . I care very much about pattern, and I want to have a beautiful shape, an apprehensible shape."[2] Murdoch believes that the problem with form, or mythic structures in fiction, is that the pattern of the novel tends to overwhelm the characters, preventing their development as complex and fully realized individuals; form can also "stop one from going more deeply into the contradictions or paradoxes or more painful aspects of the subject matter."[3] She wants to free her characters from the story, to create people with "depth and ordinariness and accidentalness," and to write fiction that, like Dickens's novels, is filled with characters who are able to escape from the constriction of a highly structured plot and to gain an importance and reality of their own. "I sometimes think," she has said, "that if I could have a novel which was made up entirely of peripheral characters, sort of accidental people like Dickens' people, this would be a very much better novel. One might go so far as starting to invent the novel and then abolishing the central characters."[4] The word *accidental*, which reappears in her statements, is important, for Murdoch believes that the realistic novelist should depict the random, contingent dimension of human life; the "form" she distrusts tends to deemphasize and simplify this aspect of reality. She maintains that there is a direct relationship between realism and contingency, and in an interview with Ronald Bryden admitted: "I would like to have much more accident in my work than I've yet managed to put in. That is, I would like to be a much more realistic novelist than I am."[5] Reality, she believes, is fragmented and often inexplicable, and the role of art is to mirror this incompleteness. In "Against Dryness" Murdoch states that "reality is not a given whole. An understanding of this, a respect for the contingent, is essential to imagination as opposed to fantasy. Our sense of form, which is an aspect of our desire for consolation, can be a danger to our sense of reality as a rich receding background."[6] She calls this background "transcendent reality," and describes it as a "sort of continuous background with a life of its own."[7] The realistic novelist should aim for as complete a rendering as is possible of the unexplainable, contingent dimension of reality and human nature, and should avoid the error of the Symbolists, who feared "history, real beings, and real change, whatever is contingent, messy, boundless, infinitely particular, and endlessly still to be explained. . . ."[8] The novelist's job is to portray the world as "aimless, chancy, and huge," and it is an error for the artist to simplify reality by attempting a rational, patterned rendering of this world.[9] In *The Sovereignty of Good over Other Concepts* Murdoch describes this godless, random world:

> I can see no evidence to suggest that human life is not something self-contained. There are properly many patterns and purposes within life, but there is no general and as it were externally guaranteed pattern or purpose of the kind for which philosophers and theologians used to search. We are what we seem to be, transient mortal creatures subject to necessity and chance. That is

> to say that there is, in my view, no God in the traditional sense of that term. . . . We are simply here.[10]

Murdoch, who believes that there is a direct relationship among comedy, contingency, and realism in fiction, has written a comic novel that embodies her vision of a random and godless world. *An Accidental Man*, a brittle comedy of manners with over twenty-four characters, contains four deaths, two attempted suicides, and characters suffering from mental retardation, schizophrenia, and brain damage. The novel is Murdoch's attempt to write fiction with a Dickensian sweep of characters and to create a world that expresses her belief in the comic nature of contingency. *An Accidental Man*, which shows Murdoch's comic skills at their best, successfully combines comedy and horror in a way that intensifies both.

At the end of the novel Matthew Gibson Grey meditates on how his brother Austin has successfully appropriated and "contaminated" Mavis Argyll, concluding that "it had all been, like so many other things in the story, accidental."[11] Like his uncle, Garth Gibson Grey is troubled by his vision of a random world ruled by contingency: "The contingent details of choice disturbed him. Everything that was offered him was too particular, not significant enough, though at the same time he realized with dazzling clarity that all decent things which human beings do are hole and corner. That was indeed, as he had told himself earlier, the point" (p. 161).[12] Charlotte Ledgard, about to commit suicide, has a similar vision of a universe ruled by chance and sees a world of "chaos upon which everything rested and out of which it was made" (p. 306). Even the uncontemplative Gracie Tisbourne is frightened by "a sense of the world being quite without order and of other things looking through" (p. 408); and Ludwig Leferrier, trying to decide what he should do about avoiding the draft, senses that "human life perches always on the brink of dissolution, and that makes all achievement empty" (p. 371). The lives of several of the characters are irrevocably altered by a bizarre series of accidents, among them Mitzi Ricardo's broken ankle, which abruptly ends her career as an athlete: "Her life had been wrecked by a momentary absurdity which it should be possible to delete" (p. 33). The deaths of Rosalind Monkley, Henrietta Sayce, and Dorina Gibson Grey are all accidental, as are Norman Monkley's fall and the resulting brain damage. It should be noted, however, that this chaotic, accidental world does not always result in tragedy, for that would endow it with a predictability that would contradict its essential nature; events such as Mavis's new spiritual awareness and Gracie's inheritance of the family fortune are also a result of chance.

Several images in the novel illustrate the accidental, inexplicable world in which the characters live. Throughout the novel Dorina is puzzled by the sentence, "*Pliez les genoux, pliez les genoux, c'est impossible de trop pliez les genoux,*" thinking that it may possibly be of religious significance. Just before her death, however, she remembers that her skiing instructor, not a holy man, had said these words to her, and the phrase's lack of profound significance exemplifies the nonsensicality and meaninglessness of phenomena in *An Accidental Man*. "So that was all that was, another senseless fragment of ownerless memory drifting about like a dead leaf" (p. 361). Several times in the novel people walk by each other without seeing or acknowledging one another, or miss meeting by moments. London's labyrinthine streets become symbolic of the ignorance and blindness of the characters as they pass and miss one another, and, in the instance of Rosalind Monkley, of accidental death itself. The two scenes of violence that haunt Garth and Matthew, appropriately called "street traumas" by Frank Baldanza, both take place on streets, one in New York and one in Moscow, and the streets of London become symbolic of the mazelike, unpredictable world in which the characters must attempt to function.[13] At the beginning of the book Matthew and Ludwig pass in the street, oblivious to one another and unaware that they will later meet and develop an important relationship. Dorina's accidental death could have been prevented had chance not prevented her from making contact with Charlotte or Austin, or if Ludwig had acknowledged seeing her on the street. Similarly, Austin's search for Dorina is *almost* successful: "Austin's intuitions were good, but temporally confused. He was often upon her track or in places which she visited on the next day. He too walked along the Serpentine, but too late. He went to the Tate Gallery, but too early. Once they were both in the same cinema at the same time, but arrived and left at different moments" (p. 359). The implication is that the characters are traveling in a maze they cannot see or understand and, as a result, are powerless to take any kind of effective action. "There's nothing to be done," says Austin. "One can't see the network" (p. 381). One of the lessons that Matthew, a more sympathetic version of Murdoch's earlier power figures, must learn is that the size and complexity of reality make control and manipulation impossible; man is not God:

> When a man has reflected much he is tempted to imagine himself as the prime author of change. Perhaps in such a mood God actually succeeded in creating the world. But for man such moods are times of illusion. What we have deeply imagined we feign to control, often with what seem to be the best of motives. But the reality is huge and dark which lies beyond the lighted area of our intentions. (P. 411)

For Murdoch, human nature and reality itself are irrational, unstructured, and unpredictable, and people who attempt to impose structures or manipulate others are acting in opposition to the nature of reality. Her belief that fiction should express the density of reality and that characters should not be overwhelmed by the story or author has its corollary in the errors the power figures in her novels make in seeking a simplication and false control of their surroundings.

Murdoch's opinion that reality is too complex for human beings to understand or control is expressed in the frustrated attempts of her characters to find consistent patterns or causal relationships in the world around them. Northrop Frye, who believes that the ironic mode, and satire in particular, often make use of this view of reality, defines satire as "the collision between a selection of standards from experience and the feeling that experience is bigger than any set of beliefs about it."[14]

The satirist, according to Frye, reveals both the futility of dictating what course of action human beings should take and the uselessness of any attempt to order or formulate a coherent scheme of what man in actuality does. Garth Gibson Grey searches for some kind of logical order and rationality in the world, but is unable to discover the "system."

> Because a child could step into the road and die there was a certain way in which it was necessary to live. The connections were there, a secret logic in the world as relentlessly necessary as a mathematical system. . . . These deaths were merely signs, accidental signs even. They were not starting points or end points. What lay before him was the system itself. . . . Absolute contradiction seemed at the heart of things and yet the system was there, the secret logic of the world, its only logic, its only sense. (Pp. 218–19)

Mavis Argyll, speaking of her sister Dorina, echoes Garth's fear that, although some sort of secret rational order exists, it is impossible for human beings to see it: "Sometimes I think it's like a puzzle and she can see and yet not quite see," says Mavis, refusing to define "it" (p. 220). Matthew, discussing with Ludwig the difficulties of achieving unselfish, unpremeditated goodness, says that the great actions of the century, such as fighting tyranny, are no longer significant: "It's more like gambling, it's roulette." It is impossible to say whether these actions have any positive effect on human life in the long run, for only "in the great web of cause and effect" that is hidden from man can this be discerned (p. 270). He mentions Gödel's theorem as an example of a system that finally must break down because it cannot prove or disprove its propositions, and disagrees with Ludwig's optimistic belief that "there must be a way through." This world of hidden meanings, unprovable propositions, and unpredictable outcomes is also, as could be expected, godless. Garth, who no longer believes in the concept of a personal God, reflects on the "rhetoric of the casually absent god" (p. 218), while Matthew, who prays not to God but to "whatever great and powerful heart might yet throb in the universe with some consciousness of good" (p. 291), thinks of his fate as arranged by "whatever deep mythological forces" control the destinies of men.

The thematic content that has been discussed so far in *An Accidental Man* would not appear to be particularly amusing. The overall tone of the novel is, nevertheless, comic, and the numerous deaths and accidents that befall the characters are for the most part viewed from a comic perspective. Frye's theory of comedy helps explain how Murdoch is able to treat this kind of dark, pessimistic subject matter in a humorous fashion, for she uses the structures of both ironic and regular comedy that Frye describes in his theory of modes. According to Frye, the theme of typical comedy (as opposed to comedy that contains elements of the ironic or romantic modes) is the integration of society and the acceptance of the comic figure. The plot structure of most modern comedy closely resembles that of Greek New Comedy, which generally presents a romantic relationship between two young people hindered by an opposing force, usually paternal. Some sort of discovery about either the hero or heroine solves the problem concerning their union, and a new society comes into being around the hero and his bride. This new society is usually controlled by youth, for the parental blocking figure has been vanquished, and the event is frequently celebrated with a party or festive ritual. As comedy moves toward the ironic mode, however, it begins to take on the darker, more pessimistic tone and structure of irony, and in its most ironic phase allows the society that has been causing problems for the hero to remain undefeated, or permits the hero, having failed to transform his society, to leave it behind. Ironic comedy also contains the comedy of manners, which Frye defines as "the portrayal of a chattering-monkey society devoted to snobbery and slander," and characteristics of the demonic world, including the expulsion of the *pharmakos*. Murdoch uses all of these elements of comedy in *An Accidental Man*, and manipulates the various comic structures for her narrative purposes.

Murdoch comes close, in *An Accidental Man*, to achieving her desire to invent a novel and then to abolish the main characters, for it is certainly a novel without a central character and conspicuously lacks any kind of hero in the traditional sense of the term. Two figures, however, can be seen to correspond to Frye's description of the comic hero. Austin Gibson Grey and Ludwig Leferrier represent, often ironically, the heroes of both the typical and ironic comedy modes that Murdoch uses to structure the novel. It is Austin who resembles in many ways the hero of the typical comic action by emerging victorious over the forces around him, while Ludwig corresponds to the hero of ironic comedy, who, in Frye's scheme, chooses to leave an unreformed society behind him. Austin, a far from sympathetic character whose actions are frequently despicable, is last seen physically and emotionally transformed into a healthy, happy individual who has used all his reversals for personal gain; ironically, this transformation is partially a result of losing his wife rather than winning a bride. Murdoch also inverts many of the conventions of the typical comic action in her treatment of Ludwig's relationship with Gracie Tisbourne. The typical comic figure usually must fight for his bride, overcoming parental or societal objections to the union, but for Ludwig the problem is that everything is simply too *easy*. The book begins with Gracie's acceptance of his proposal and the delight of her parents, events quickly followed by his receiving a teaching appointment at Oxford. Instead of Gracie's inheritance coming about so that the heroine can be made respectable or acceptable and the marriage can be performed, as in traditional comedy, her windfall occurs after her engagement and is simply one more aspect of the couple's idyllic situation. The blocking *senex* figure is instead Ludwig's father and the government of the United States: his father wants him to terminate his engagement and return home to gain conscientious objector status so that he can avoid fighting in Vietnam. Instead of the novel's ending with the expected wedding of Gracie and Ludwig, he decides to leave his bride-to-be and a rosy future in England, opting for a return to the United States and the prison term that awaits him. The newly married couple at the end is instead Garth and Gracie, and the party that concludes the story is an ironic version of the "festival" that Frye speaks of as the typical ending of the comic action. Murdoch inverts the structure of typical comedy and uses elements of ironic comedy in her treatment of the fortunes of Austin and Ludwig, and by doing so creates an extremely complex comic structure that defeats the reader's generic expectations. Murdoch also reverses the comic convention of the triumph of youth over age in her portraits of Ludwig and Austin. It is the middle-aged Austin rather than the twenty-two-year-old Ludwig who is successful and rejuvenated at the end of the story; Ludwig, on the other hand, bows to the wishes of his father. The deaths of the two young children in the novel, Henrietta Sayce and Rosalind Monkley, are another aspect of this, for in this world young people appear to be more vulnerable to the vicissitudes of fortune than their elders. In another sense, however, youth is in control throughout the novel, and there is no movement from one kind of society to another; in fact, one comic element in *An Accidental Man* is the fact that many of the young people are more sophisticated, articulate, and intelligent than their elders. Clara and George Tisbourne, both comically in awe of their two children, illustrate this, as do the personalities of Patrick and Gracie.

Another characteristic of ironic comedy is the presence of the *pharmakos*, an individual who must be driven out of the society to insure its continued existence and vitality. Dorina Gibson Grey is the most obvious scapegoat character in all of Murdoch's fiction. Dorina, who sees herself as hounded and pursued by others, observes that "it was as if something were closing in for the kill" (p. 98), and several of the characters believe that they benefit by her death. Matthew describes Dorina as a "hunted creature," a "captive," and Austin, because of his paranoid fears, wishes to keep his wife "immobilized and spellbound" in Mavis's home. Many of the characters feel that Dorina needs to be dealt with in some way, and Mavis and Matthew in particular wish her to leave Valmorana so that they can be free to resume their affair. Dorina is also described as having close affinities with the occult, an aspect of her personality that is treated comically at one point in the novel: "There had been strange incidents. 'I am afraid your sister attracts poltergeists,' one headmistress had complained severely to Mavis, who had her own ghosts to contend with" (p. 57). The schizophrenic Dorina's delusions are not treated comically, however, and the scenes in her hotel room before her death are a chilling depiction of a mentally ill person attempting to remain sane.

Mavis, Garth, and Austin all feel that Dorina's death has been, in a sense, a positive event that has had beneficial effects on their personal lives. Mavis tells Matthew that "I cannot help feeling that she somehow died for us, for you and me, taking herself away, clearing herself away, so that our world should be easier and simpler" (p. 400). Mavis later meditates that "she has died for me," and says that "Dorina's departure had released her into some sort of vast beyond" (p. 423). Dorina's death causes Garth to make a vital contact with his past, which in turn enables him again to feel love for his father: "Her death had this use for him, that a stream flowed again between himself and the past and after being dry-eyed for many years he was able to weep again." The result of this is a renewed interest in himself and the rebirth of affectionate feelings for Austin; the narrator says that "love for his father possessed his body like a memory" (p. 374). Significantly, the policeman arrives at this moment to return his lost novel, for it is almost as if Garth's creative potential is restored by Dorina's death. Austin, who describes his wife's death as a "felicitous solution," rejoices that her death has isolated her from the influences of other people and has insured that she cannot hurt him. In fact, Austin's rejuvenation is apparently due, to a degree, to the death of his wife, as Matthew clearly realizes: "Something or other had, in however ghastly a sense, done Austin 'good.' Perhaps it was simply Dorina's death" (p. 432). Dorina is a character who, partially because of her mental instability and lack of egocentricity, must be cast out of the society of the novel, a society that can accommodate only such characters as Mavis, Austin, and Garth; the strong survival instincts of these individuals guarantee their ability to endure and recover from catastrophes. Dorina's death has positive effects on each of these characters and corresponds to the "point of ritual death" that Frye describes as a typical event of ironic comedy, and both her expulsion from society and her connection with the occult show her to be a character of that mode.

An early indication of the tone of *An Accidental Man* is evident when Charlotte Ledgard telephones her sister to report that their mother is dying. "Oh God. We're dining with the Arbuthnots," replies Clara (p. 37). At the end of the novel, though extremely upset over Henrietta Sayce's death, her thoughts return to money and matchmaking as she grieves: "I used to think sometimes she might make a wife for Patrick when she grew up, they were so fond of each other, and there's all that money on Penny's side, and now she's dead, oh dear, dear, dear—" (p. 412). The death of Alison Ledgard is one of the most sustained comic scenes in Murdoch's fiction, a scene in which the nurse's primping and Clara's worry about a possible "legal snag" over the inheritance take precedence over the fact of death itself. The doctor's lack of interest in his patient and the clergyman's forced and cliché-filled death prayer add to the comedy; Dr. Seldon makes a point of advising the family that there is no need to call him in the event of Alison's death, and Enstone appears to be more involved with ping-pong at the Youth Club. The comic technique used in this passage is obviously Freud's idea of the "economy of sympathy," a process by which the emphasis is taken away from the painful aspects of a situation and attention is redirected to an area less painful. Charlotte alone appears to be sensitive to the reality of her mother's death, and the narrator chooses to place the pathetic and sorrowful dimensions of the event in the background. Dying is treated comically not because it is intrinsically funny, but because of the selfishness and greed of the living juxtaposed to the finality of death.

Alison's death and funeral are later used for comic purposes by other characters in the novel. In a letter to Gracie, Patrick refers to the "funeral games. I hope you enjoy them. Poor old Grandma. Everyone will be rejoicing, won't they, especially Aunt Char. What news of the carve-up?" (p. 73). Gracie's reply to her brother, which begins "Grandma's funeral was a riot, I wish you'd been there" (p. 78), later casually characterizes her father as taking the funeral in a "literary sense." She also mentions that her Aunt Charlotte looks twenty years younger and describes the festivities that followed the funeral in this manner:

> You see, everyone stood around for a while trying to be solemn, and then we heard a burst of gay laughter from the kitchen where Papa and Sir Charles had opened a bottle of champagne. Then we all converged on the kitchen and there were drinks all round, and people were sitting on the kitchen table and draped round the hall stairs with glasses in their hands and corks were popping, it was quite a wake. (P. 79)

Gracie, who rarely allows surrounding disasters to discomfit her, also describes Norman Monkley's fall down Austin's stairs, which results in permanent brain damage, as "another jolly disaster" (p. 245). Not surprisingly in a novel in which characters view death and disaster with such jovial equanimity, Norman's partial "recovery" is treated comically, and both Austin's phony concern for Norman and Mrs. Monkley's appreciation of it become ironically humorous in light of what the reader knows about the true facts of the "accident." The narrator concludes this section of the novel with a statement that aptly exemplifies the tone of *An Accidental Man:* "The hospital staff now thought that Norman would never fully recover. So that was all very satisfactory" (p. 319).

Patrick's reaction to the death of Rosalind Monkley is similar:

> So Austin has run over a little girl. Good for him. He has certainly maximized happiness in the Tisbourne family. Ma was incoherent with delight about it when she telephoned and I could just imagine her face, pulled into that false sadness with glee looking through. And don't tell me you don't feel exactly the same. I would be moderately bucked myself if I hadn't got other troubles. As it is, I wake up in the morning and feel at once that at least *something* nice has happened. (P. 180)

Patrick Tisbourne actually emerges as a fairly sympathetic character in the novel, for he openly acknowledges the feelings the other characters attempt to hide. While Margaret Scanlon's description of him as the "sober moral arbiter" of the novel is rather exaggerated, his unabashedly truthful analyses of people and events do have a moral dimension.[15] The Tisbournes, however, are not alone in their enjoyment of the troubles of others. The fact that many of the characters in *An Accidental Man* wholeheartedly enjoy the misfortunes of other people is a recurring comic motif, and the pleasure is usually intensified when the "victims" are close friends or family members. Mitzi glories in Austin's marital difficulties, and Mavis finds pleasure in Dorina's problems with Austin. Mrs. Monkley's tragedies are, for Garth, "a bit exciting. It was life-giving, even pleasurable" (p. 206); in the same way Matthew finds Ludwig's troubles "thoroughly exhilarating." In a scene reminiscent of the group assembled around Georgie Hands's hospital bed in *A Severed Head,* Mitzi informs Charlotte that her visitors were "thrilled" by her suicide attempt. Patrick Tisbourne's statements in his letters make him the most truthful and objective of the characters.

Characters do not limit themselves to a simple enjoyment of other people's catastrophes; rather, they often utilize them for their own purposes. Andrew Hilton uses the suicide attempt of a pupil as an excuse to begin a sexual relationship, telling Oliver Sayce in a letter that "my ablest pupil has just attempted suicide. I must go and surround him with affection" (p. 327). In the same way, the hoped-for renewal of the relationship between Matthew and Mavis, which fails miserably over lunch and drinks, suddenly blooms in an automobile after both have paid a visit to the disconsolate Mrs. Monkley. The narrator's refusal to treat any human problem with sustained sympathy, an important aspect of the novel that deepens its comic tone, is also evident in the scenes between Matthew and Charlotte, and Charlotte and Mitzi. Charlotte is treated dismissively by Matthew when she tells of her lifelong love for him, and the exact phrases of their conversation are repeated in the parallel scene in which Charlotte attempts to leave Mitzi, a repetition that reduces the importance of the characters' emotions and in the process renders them comic. Scenes that are potentially emotionally explosive, rather than being presented as uniquely important events, are trivialized by being made to seem stereotyped and cliché-filled. There are few subjects in *An Accidental Man* that are not comically reduced or treated ironically, a humorous treatment of subject matter that is increased by the lack of narrative information in many scenes, particularly in the epistolary chapters.

One of the most important comic dimensions of *An Accidental Man* is the attitude of the narrator: the absence of narrative comment and information at certain points in the novel becomes a comic device. The tone is one of detachment and distance from many of the horrible events described, and the narrator's gradually expanding vision of people and situations helps create the comic perspective of the narrative. Chapters consisting solely of letters written from one character to another and chapters of untagged dialogue also serve to eliminate the presence of a narrating voice. Murdoch has stated her wish to expel herself from her fiction, to avoid imposing "the form of one's own mind" on the characters, and *An Accidental Man* is one of her most successful attempts at eliminating authorial presence. Individuals are frequently seen and heard from the outside, for the narrator does not reveal the reactions or thoughts of the characters in several important dramatic scenes, and the reader is called upon to contribute the information. Again, Freud gives an insight into why this lack of narrative is funny: his theory of the "principle of economy" in jokes helps explain why forcing the reader or listener to arrive at a conclusion or understanding without a full explanation is often a humorous technique. This is not to say that the narrator is always absent, however, for in a scene in which Charlotte and Mavis attempt to persuade Dorina to leave Valmorana the narrator creates a comic counterpoint between the polite social conversations of the characters and the far different reality of their thoughts (pp. 145–48), a technique used again in the luncheon scene between Matthew and Mavis.

Several of the novel's most comic scenes are rendered dramatically through dialogue only; the narrator does not provide the additional information the reader generally expects from onmiscient narration. In the final confrontation between Austin and Matthew, the comedy is a result of the reader's prior knowledge of Matthew's personality, a knowledge that enables the reader to guess Matthew's real thoughts as he makes the short replies to his recently rejuvenated brother. Austin, speaking of the brain-damaged Norman Monkley, does most of the talking, and Matthew's complete disgust with his brother's transformation is brilliantly presented through indirection and irony:

> "I went to see the Monkleys last week. Norman was doing some sort of basket work. He's quite a sweet character now."
> "Good."
> "I must fly. I've got to get over to the flat, and I said I'd cook supper for Mavis. She'll be exhausted. She's been spending today carting the char's idiot child to an institution."
> "Mavis is very kind."
> "Yes, isn't she. You know, her kindness to me has been an absolute revelation. I felt such a miserable wreck and she's quite put me on my feet again. I must say I had a rotten time. But now I feel like a re-constituted Humpty Dumpty."
> "She's good at helping."
> "You can say that again. You know, she's awfully like Dorina in a way, she's got that concentrated sweetness, but without any of the feyness and fear. I don't think Mavis is afraid of anything."
> "No, indeed,"
> "Poor old Dorina was just a sort of half person really, a maimed creature, she had to die, like certain kinds of cripples have to. They can't last."
> "Maybe."
> "That idiot child will probably die in its teens, the doctor told Mavis. A good thing too. Mavis didn't tell the mother, of course."
> "Naturally—"
> "Mavis has certainly helped me to see the world in perspective."
> "I'm glad." (P. 410)

Austin's first appearance in the novel is presented in much the same way, but in this instance Murdoch's technical feat is more impressive because neither of the characters in the scene has appeared before. The reader begins to identify with Austin and to realize, without help from the narrator, his reaction to his dismissal:

> "Recession. Yes," said Austin Gibson Grey. He was not sure what recession meant, but he knew what Mr. Bransome meant.
> "It is a matter of computerization."
> "Indeed."
> "There is nothing personal involved."
> "Quite."
> "The management consultants who were here last month—"
> "I thought they were interior decorators."
> "Possibly they were so described."
> "They were."
> "It was a matter of being tactful."
> "I see."
> "Recommended a thoroughgoing streamlining of staff ratios."
> "Ah, yes."
> "You appreciate that we have been losing money."
> "I do."
> "Our situation, I say in confidence, is difficult."
> "I am sorry."
> "We shall pay you of course for the entire month."
> "Thank you."
> "But I trust you will feel free to leave at any time."
> "How kind." (P. 16)

The cocktail-party chapters are handled in a similar fashion. Murdoch presents pages of untagged one-liners that create what Frye so aptly calls the "chattering-monkey society" of ironic comedy, leaving the reader to try to ascertain the identities of the speakers and to piece together the relationships among the characters. By this time, however, the reader knows more about the events of the novel than any of the characters. For example, in the first of these chapters (pp. 130–36) the reader's earlier knowledge of Oliver Sayce's homosexuality causes his first encounter with Andrew Hilton to have a comic dimension dependent on this knowledge, just as Mavis's questioning of Charlotte about Matthew is amusing because the reader has been informed of the reason for her interest. Murdoch also uses these chapters to reduce important events that were treated seriously in earlier episodes to comically trivial cocktail-party conversation. Charlotte, whose unhappiness has been sympathetically treated for the most part, is turned into a figure of fun:

> "Isn't that Charlotte Ledgard?"
> "I thought she'd run away to sea."
> "She only ran as far as Bailey's Hotel." (P. 132)

The long-delayed meeting between Matthew and Austin, which the reader has expected to occupy an important place in the narrative, is reduced to five lines:

> "Oh hello, Austin."
> "Hello, Matthew."
> "Your job must be very interesting too, Mr. Enstone."
> "How about a drink sometime soon, Austin?"
> "Sorry, Matthew, I'm just leaving town." (P. 134)

The party chapters and epistolary sections are an important comical dimension of the novel, for Murdoch uses them to advance the narrative through fragmentary bits of information that are often necessary for a complete understanding of what is happening; her belief that "reality is not a given whole" is expressed in her narrative technique. The reader is given fragmented insights into the characters and situations, but is almost always in the position of knowing more than the characters, a position that creates a comic irony directly related to the lack of direct information from the narrator. The disappearance of the narrator in certain sections of the novel parallels the beliefs of the characters in the absence of god; it is as if Murdoch wishes to create a novelistic world in which the reader must search for his own patterns and conclusions without the guiding presence of the author. The narrator's refusal to pass judgments or to give information about the thoughts of characters, despite the fact that he has shown himself to be omniscient, results in a coldly detached tone that refuses to grant a fundamental importance to any act. Margaret Scanlon believes that the novel is flawed because the reader is denied an explanation of Ludwig's decision to leave England, and she says that "we are not sufficiently involved in his mind to perceive the gradual enlargement of vision that impells the return home."[16] This, however, is a deliberate stratagem on Murdoch's part: the failure to give the reader a complete account of Ludwig's motives is one aspect of the comic perspective of the narrator, which partially depends upon his distance and detachment from the events of the narrative. Because of this it is not surprising that the reader, like Ludwig's parents, is suddenly notified of his decision to return to America by a telegram at the conclusion of an epistolary chapter: "FATHER PLEASE CANCEL YOUR SAILING I AM COMING HOME LUDWIG" (p. 401).

At times the narrator seems to disappear from *An Accidental Man*, and this lack of narrative presence is most evident in the epistolary chapters, which consist solely of letters written from one character to another, chapters that make up over ten percent of the novel. Like the chapters of dialogue, these sections create a voyeuristic situation for the reader, in which he is privileged to read correspondence and to overhear conversations. Voyeurism, a recurrent theme throughout Murdoch's fiction, is a very important motif in *An Accidental Man*, and the characters have a noticeable penchant for eavesdropping and reading other people's letters. Matthew listens outside Austin's door, Austin overhears his son lecturing Ludwig, and Dorina stumbles in on her husband about to make love to Mitzi Ricardo. In the same way Austin reads Dorina's letter to Ludwig, Norman steals Matthew's letter to Austin, and Charlotte discovers Betty's note to Matthew.

As in the dialogue chapters, comically ironic effects are created because the reader knows more about the entire situation than do the individual letter writers. In light of the reader's knowledge of Patrick's homosexuality, Hester Odmore's hope that Patrick will be a "steadying influence" on her son is comic, as is Matthew's entreaty to the unrepentant

Austin not to be "filled with grief" and blame himself for Rosalind's death. Clara, unaware that her sister has attempted suicide, writes to Hester that "Charlotte seems reasonably okay, in fact she has gone away on holiday. We are doing our best to cheer her along" in a letter that is darkly comic (p. 322). It has been noted that Murdoch is interested in the way people use language to lie and distort the truth, and Murdoch's letter writers in *An Accidental Man* are adept at protective verbal manipulation. Austin's first letter to Dorina, filled with outright lies about how he lost his job, what Mitzi charges for rent, and his first meeting with Matthew, is one of the most comical letters in the novel. Clara Tisbourne's letter to Hester Odmore about Gracie's condition after her break-up with Ludwig, in which she describes her daughter as "quite restored and gay," becomes extremely humorous in light of the content of her next letter to Dr. Seldon: "She still refuses to eat and lies all day on her bed crying and talks a good deal about suicide" (p. 397). This kind of comic juxtaposition is used throughout, for Murdoch will often switch abruptly from a scene of horror, such as Rosalind Monkley's death or Norman's fall, to a series of comic letters, changes in tone that disorient the reader and call into question the seriousness of the events of the novel. Murdoch, who has said that the artist must aim for a depiction of "death without a consolation," denies the reader the consolation of a consistently serious attitude toward the novel's terrible events.

The epistolary chapters also give Murdoch a chance to expand the boundaries of her fictive world, to include, as she has stated she wishes to do, more and more peripheral characters. The reader becomes increasingly interested in the sexual adventures of various individuals, many of whom are not involved in the main action of the book. In these chapters the reader sees Patrick conquer Ralph Odmore's objections to a homosexual relationship, Karen Arbuthnot plan and succeed in marrying Sebastian Odmore, and Andrew Hilton and Oliver Sayce begin and develop their love affair. All these liaisons are humorous because of their indirect presentation through letters; the reader is given a sense of an almost limitless potential in the novel, an ever-expanding view of persons and interrelationships that corresponds to Murdoch's desire to write fiction that depicts "reality as a rich receding background," a "continuous background with a life of its own." The widening framework of the novel contributes to its comic dimensions by creating a constantly changing perspective: as the narrator pulls back from a direct presentation of events, as in the case of the automobile accident or Norman's fall, to the reactions of peripheral and uninvolved characters, the importance of the events is reduced through distancing and in the process is rendered comic. For example, Rosalind Monkley's death, which is first presented dramatically and is meant to have an emotional impact on the reader, is followed by a chapter of letters in which the incident is relegated to a P.S. in Karen Arbuthnot's humorous letter to Sebastian Odmore: "Did you hear that Austin Gibson Grey ran over a child? I am so sorry for that man. I think he is in love with Gracie, incidentally. What a planet" (p. 181). The death of a child becomes less and less important as the reader moves into the worlds of minor characters, what Frank Baldanza calls the "shadow novel" in *An Accidental Man*.[17] Murdoch again transforms the serious into the comical when Austin overhears his son's conversation with Ludwig, for when the reader hears a portion of Garth's lecture for the second time, this time from Austin's point of view, the perspective is changed and Garth appears pompous and ridiculous.

Austin Gibson Grey has several of the characteristics of the comic hero, including a talent for survival, resilience, and the ability to manipulate the people around him. Austin is the self-acknowledged accidental man of the book's title; "I am an accidental man," he tells Mavis, who tries to comfort him by saying that we are all accidental people. "With me it's gone on and on," replies Austin (p. 424). It is true that although events transpire to place Austin in unfortunate situations, his callousness and resilience allow him, as Mavis observes, to turn all his accidents to account. Austin, one of the most invidious characters in Murdoch's fiction, nevertheless has a sense of irony and detachment from his own life, and his sometimes ironic perceptions of himself cause the reader to temper the disapprobation his actions and attitudes merit. Murdoch's portrayal of Austin has a decidedly comic dimension that shows her once again choosing to present human failings in a humorous light, a choice that parallels her comic treatment of the power figures in the later novels. Though Scanlon calls Austin a "monster" and Mavis admits that he is a "vampire," he is merely the most exaggerated example of human egotism and solipsism in *An Accidental Man*, and the statement at the end of the novel that "Austin is like all of us only more so" is appropriate in the context of the novel's world (p. 440).

Comic characters are often endowed with an egotistical nature that the action of the comedy will either correct or vindicate. Although Austin realizes his inability to "rise upon . . . humiliations to higher things" in the moral realm, his egotism is his means of survival, as Mitzi learns (p. 18):

> Austin helped Mitzi by a revelation of how it was possible to live simply by egoism. Austin, with nothing particular to boast of, never seemed to doubt his own absolute importance. Just because he was himself the world owed him everything, and even though the world paid him very little, he remained a sturdy and vociferous creditor. Misery could not crush Austin. Simply being Austin enabled him to carry on. (P. 34)

Austin, more self-consciously bent on his own survival than any other character in the book, realizes that appealing to Matthew for help from Norman's blackmail would break his "springs of survival," and the narrator observes that Austin is aware that often "a man can see himself becoming more callous because he has to survive" (p. 157). This growing callousness to events is evident in his letter to Dorina about the death of Rosalind Monkley: "I am *all right* and I will survive and recover, I have had worse blows than this" (p. 179), and he later tells Mavis that "I've got to survive—that's what my will's been for—" (p. 383).[18]

One characteristic of Austin's ability to survive is his refusal to allow the tragedies of others to touch him. After Norman's accident he falls into a sound sleep; his reaction to his wife's death is similar. His first thoughts about Alison Ledgard's death are also predictable: "So the old woman was gone. Good. Charlotte would be rich and would lend him money" (p. 50). In fact, in keeping with Austin's propensity for turning unfortunate happenings to personal gain, his search for his missing wife becomes such a pleasurable experience that he often forgets her entirely. Dorina's death is for Austin a "felicitous solution," which he uses as a catalyst for his own rejuvenation. At the conclusion of the novel the reader witnesses the figurative "rebirth of the hero" that several comic theoreticians discuss, and, in fact, Austin's acknowledgment of his "accidental" existence and talent for overcoming misfortune make Langer's description of the comic action as the "upset and recovery of the protagonist's equilibrium, his contest with the world and his triumph by wit, luck, personal power, or even humorous, or ironical, or philosophical acceptance of mischance" a fitting one for *An Accidental Man.*[19] Austin's ironical acceptance of his own plight also gives him a much-needed attractive quality; his sense of humor is particularly evident in the comic scenes in which Norman Monkley attempts to blackmail him into reading and criticizing his novel.

One of his more negative traits is his skill in manipulating the people around him. Mitzi and Dorina are especially dominated by him, and he succeeds in finally vanquishing the specter of his brother, in the process, as Scanlon observes, turning Mavis into a replica of Dorina, a feat that "contaminates" her in Matthew's eyes and ruins all possibilities for their future relationship. The final scene of the novel, in which Austin is finally able to move his fingers, underscores his final victory over the forces that have plagued him, for his inability to use his hand since his childhood "accident" has been symbolic throughout the novel of his problems in dealing with the world. His new physical flexibility parallels the rebirth of his personality, brought about, as previously noted, by the misfortunes of other people.

The final section of *An Accidental Man*, with its emphasis on Austin's rejuvenation and acceptance by society, with the pairings of couples and the resulting pregnancies of Ann Colindale, Gracie, and Karen, and with the cocktail-party setting, would seem to be an example of the typical ending of comedy discussed by Northrop Frye. However, the novel ends on the same darkly comic note that has been its tone throughout, and because several factors cause this "festive party" ending to be less than celebratory, Frye's description of the conclusion of ironic comedy is much more applicable here. For a number of characters, the action of the novel has brought about a realization of personal failure. Matthew, sailing to America with Ludwig, realizes that "he would never be a hero. . . . He would be until the end of his life a man looking forward to his next drink. He looked at his watch and drifted down to the bar" (p. 436). Garth's marriage to Gracie is another admission of failure; like Matthew, he has searched and failed to find some sort of moral pattern. Though the reader does not see the process by which Garth is transformed from a philosophically oriented social worker to a sleek, successful novelist and party-giver, it is obvious he has decided to settle for the comfortable, shallow existence represented by Gracie and her social set. Garth's answers to Gracie's questions before the party reveal him to be satisfied and happy with his new life-style, and his apparent discovery of Gracie's secret nickname, "Moggie," is humorously noted by the narrator: it would appear that Garth is willing and eager to share what Gracie has earlier called her "talent for happiness." The acceptance of failure by Matthew and Garth can be contrasted with the positive transformations of Austin and Clara Tisbourne, both of whom are described as looking younger in the final pages of the novel. The fact that both these individuals, unsympathetically presented throughout the narrative, have apparently survived unscathed and used the horror around them for personal betterment is described by the narrator from an externally objective point of view. "Clara was now wearing her hair straight and rather short. She looked radiantly juvenile. So did Austin, his copious golden locks flowing down onto his collar. He never wore glasses now. His contact lenses were a great success" (p. 437).

The final party section of *An Accidental Man* is characterized by the same dark, ominous tone that was present throughout the novel. Presided over by Mary Monkley, now the Gibson Greys' cleaning woman, this section contains the information that Ludwig Leferrier has been sent to prison in America, a fact that is casually mentioned by one party-goer and quickly dropped. Just as valuable and meaningful information and events were reduced to triviality and absurdity in earlier sections of the novel, so Ludwig's fate, the real moral dilemma of the story, is treated as less important than Gracie's arrangement of cushions on the sofa. In fact, Ludwig's problem is not even stated correctly by the guest, who, when asked why he is in prison, answers, "Drugs or something" (p. 439). The society depicted at the conclusion of the novel is one in which the external, social aspects of existence take precedence over morality and truth. In four lines of dialogue Murdoch expresses the brittle tone and hypocrisy of the upper-middle-class liberal milieu she has created in *An Accidental Man:*

> "Clara will soon be Lady Tisbourne."
> "Mollie will soon be Lady Arbuthnot."
> "Aren't we all getting grand."
> "Anyway, we're still socialists." (P. 440)

She shows, in the differing descriptions of Patrick Tisbourne's reactions to Charlotte's new living arrangement, how the truth and unique importance of human relationships are distorted and rendered ridiculous by outsiders. Charlotte's earlier realization that a knowledge of the truth about reality leads not to happiness but to "some final bitter wit" can be seen as important here, for the novel ends on a bitterly comic note that is a result of both its form and content. In this final sequence, unlike the earlier chapters of dialogue and letters, the reader becomes less and less sure who is speaking; the disembodied voices create an ominous atmosphere from which the narrator *and* major characters seem to have departed, leaving the reader alone to eavesdrop on the chattering of strangers. Frye's theory that the most ironic phase of comedy is one in which a humorous society triumphs or remains undefeated best describes the situation at the end of *An Accidental Man*, for the society that is in control in the final pages of the novel has accepted its "accidental man," expelled its *pharmakos*, and remains devoted to snobbery and slander.

4

The Artist as *Eiron* in *The Black Prince*

In *An Accidental Man* the most important comic technique is the attitude of the novel's omniscient narrator, who frequently withdraws from commenting on events, allowing the reader to infer the proper information and/or reaction. In *The Black Prince* Murdoch uses first person narration, as in *Under the Net* and *A Severed Head*, for comic effects: in this novel, the comic dimension is created by Bradley Pearson's attitude toward and presentation of the events of his narrative. Ronald Wallace has noted that first person narration has become increasingly popular as a comic device in contemporary fiction because of the comic potential of "unconscious self-exposure . . . when the hero himself is cast as the narrator of his own fiction,"[1] a situation in which the narrator may attempt to lie to the reader, may himself remain deluded throughout the story, or may lack the critical detachment necessary to tell his story truthfully. In any case, the ironic discrepancy that results from the reader's realization that the narrator is manipulating the narrative for his own purposes is a comic device. Wallace makes another important point in his study of modern comic fiction that is relevant to an analysis of *The Black Prince* as a comic novel, for, like *An Accidental Man*, the novel contains events that are not generally considered comical, including a suicide, a murder, and the death of the narrator. Wallace's statement that "it is not the subject matter, but the author's attitude toward it that determines the tragic or comic basis of a literary form"[2] correctly describes the narrative technique Murdoch uses in the novel: Bradley Pearson's attitude toward the events he narrates, essentially comic throughout, combines an ironical apprehension of the world outside himself with a self-mocking tone to create a novel in which the comic mode predominates despite the sometimes tragic nature of the subject matter.

Several views of Bradley Pearson are given in *The Black Prince*, for Murdoch adds five postscripts by characters who have appeared earlier, each of whom comments on Bradley and qualifies his interpretation and presentation of the events. Described as a victim by his editor, P. Loxias, and a buffoon by Rachel Baffin, Bradley plays a variety of roles in *The Black Prince:* ironic narrator, buffoon, self-styled "possessed artist," and scapegoat. Wylie Sypher has observed that it is not unusual for the comic hero, unlike the tragic hero, to function as several different types of characters, and Bradley clearly corresponds to a description of the comic character that stresses his ability to assume any number of *personae*. Francis Cornford, who discusses the structure of ancient comedy as a debate between the *eiron* and *alazon*, speaks of the "mocking Irony of the hero, who draws out the Impostor's absurdities and sets them at naught,"[3] but also says that "the Buffoon and the *eiron* are more closely allied in Aristotle's view than a modern reader might expect."[4] Sypher, like Cornford, describes the comic hero as having a dual nature as both ironist and buffoon and believes his personality can include elements of the *pharmakos* and the prophet or possessed seer.[5] Northrop Frye's description of ironic comedy, as discussed earlier, includes a character who abandons society and becomes a kind of *pharmakos* figure in reverse, or a hero whom society views as a fool; the real audience, on the other hand, is aware that this individual is more valuable than the society that scorns him. The various dimensions of Bradley's personality become understandable in light of the tendency of the comic character to play a variety of roles, and, given the elastic, expansive structure of comedy, it is not surprising that the comic novel can contain a detached ironical narrator who also functions as buffoon, scapegoat, and artist-figure during the course of the narrative.

The Black Prince, like *An Accidental Man*, includes some of the archetypal structures of Old and New Comedy, though Murdoch continues to invert typical comic structures for ironic purposes. *The Black Prince* contains a modernized version of the ancient debates between the *eiron* and *alazon* in the form of Bradley's arguments about art and novel writing with the "impostor artist," Arnold Baffin, and Murdoch also inverts the typical structure of romantic comedy, which generally presents a young man and woman who wish to marry but are temporarily prevented, usually by the *senex* or "heavy father" figure. In *The Black Prince* the "young man" of typical comedy is replaced by the fifty-eight-year-old narrator, who is ten years older than the *senex* figure, Arnold Baffin. In the scene at Patara, Arnold plays the classic role of the *senex iratus*, angrily denouncing Bradley as a "filthy lustful old man" and threatening to take Julian out of the country for her own protection.

This structure is further complicated by the incestuous connotations of the situation, for although Bradley does not have a blood relationship with Julian, he says he feels like a "spiritual father" to Arnold, a relationship that places him in a tenuous position in regard to the young woman who is already young enough to be his daughter. In his discussion of comedy Frye notes that the "possibility" of an incestuous combination is one of the minor themes of comedy, and Murdoch allows incestuous relationships to go beyond being mere "possibilities" in several novels, particularly *A Severed Head* and *The Time of the Angels*. Frye also mentions that the son and father are frequently in conflict because they are rivals for the same young girl, a situation that has its corollary in *The Black Prince* when Julian is forced to choose between Bradley and her father at Patara; later, when traveling on the Continent with Arnold, she writes Bradley that people believe that she and her father are lovers and adds that "perhaps he is *the* man in my life!" (p. 320),[6] a statement that underscores the way in which Murdoch is using both incestuous innuendo and the structures of Greek and Roman comedy. Murdoch also inverts the structure of traditional comedy by having the lovers in *The Black Prince* remain permanently separated, although Bradley's subtitle for his novel, *A Celebration of Love*, is nonetheless appropriate, for his finished work is the artistic achievement that panegyrizes his affair with Julian. Wallace's belief that "parody has the unique capability of simultaneously ridiculing and affirming the form and assumptions of its original," and that by parodying sexual activity the comic novelist simultaneously ridicules and celebrates the subject matter, is pertinent for *The Black Prince*, which presents Bradley's love affair from a comic and serious perspective as both celebration and fiasco.[7]

In addition to functioning as the angry father of typical romantic comedy, the popular novelist Arnold Baffin also plays the role of *alazon*, an artistic impostor who, in the words of his daughter, writes novels that portray "Jesus and Mary and Buddha and Shiva and the Fisher King all chasing round and round dressed up as people in Chelsea" (p. 110). Cornford says that the *alazons* of ancient comedy are "all of them touched with some form of pretentiousness, swagger, conceit, which makes them ridiculous and incurs the irony of the hero-buffoon";[8] they are absurd, boastful, and impudent pretenders, usually of the professional class, who are cast in the role of quack or humbug and generally function as unwelcome intruders who interrupt some sort of religious or social event. The structure of the comic action, which often consists of a dramatized debate between the *alazon* and *eiron*, appears in *The Black Prince* in the form of the conversations between Bradley and Arnold. These discussions usually result in arguments about the creative process, with the self-confident novel-a-year-writer Baffin doing most of the talking while Bradley plays the role of the ironically restrained artist who refuses to pander to popular taste. Bradley, like Matthew Gibson Grey in *An Accidental Man*, usually gives short, ironic answers which make Arnold appear effusive and foolish, a habit that causes Arnold rightly to accuse him of taking "refuge in irony." Arnold, like the *alazons* of ancient comedy, often invades Bradley's physical surroundings and/or consciousness, and he is characterized by Bradley as a kind of quack-artist who has sacrificed real aesthetic achievement for money and fame. Arnold's resemblance to the *alazon* figure is further evidenced by Francis Marloe's postscript statement that Arnold functioned as Bradley's *alter ego*, for the *alazon* often acts as the *alter ego* of the *eiron*.

The third major character of ancient comedy, the buffoon, is represented in the novel by Francis Marloe. Cornford says that if the comic hero is more *eiron* than buffoon, the role of "buffoonery pure and simple" is frequently played by "a subordinate character, in some way attached to the hero as friend or attendant,"[9] and Frye notes that the oldest buffoon character is the parasite. Bradley begins his narrative by describing Francis as the "page or housemaid" of the tale, and he remains a comic parasite throughout the novel, begging for money and liquor, sobbing over his homosexuality, and continually bustling around Bradley's home in attempts to be helpful. Even his postscript fails to give him a serious dimension, for his wildly exaggerated Freudian interpretation of Bradley's novel is extremely comic, as are his attempts to market his own writings and to attract new patients. Francis's peripheral importance is underscored by Bradley's statement in the foreword that "poor Francis will never be the hero of anything. He would make an excellent fifth wheel to any coach. But I make him as it were the mascot of the tale, partly because in a purely mechanical sense he opens it" (p. xiv), and, although the other characters in the novel are treated with varying degrees of seriousness in different situations, Francis's role remains, in Cornford's words, that of "subordinate buffoon."

Bradley's most important role is that of the *eiron*, and his ironic sensibility structures and sets the tone of the entire novel. A self-mocking ironist, he openly admits to being nervous and neurotic from the very beginning of the story, readily acknowledging his own fears and obsessions. In fact, his honesty is one of his most likable characteristics, and it enables the reader to accept more easily his devastating portraits of the other characters. Describing himself in the early pages of the novel as "a man who never went anywhere," he introduces himself to the reader in a comic scene in which his neurotic fears force him to unpack and repack suitcases because he is terrified at the thought of leaving anything behind. Shortly thereafter he characterizes himself as "dazed with success" at being able to throw away slivers of soap in the bathroom, confesses that he suffers from insomnia and stomach trouble, and admits to an abnormal fear of trains, theaters, crowds, and orchestras. Bradley uses his eccentricity and misanthropy for humorous purposes, simultaneously revealing his phobias and anxieties while using inflated diction which signals to the reader that he is well aware of the comical figure he is cutting. The description of his reaction to trains is typical. "Trains induce such terrible anxiety. They image the possibility of total and irrevocable failure. They are also dirty, rackety, packed with strangers, an object lesson in the foul contingency of life: the talkative fellow-traveller, the possibility of children" (p. 44); and his paranoid description of music as "a sinister gabbling in a language one can almost understand, a gabbling which is horribly, one suspects, *about onself*" is another example of this technique (p. 218). His detailed description of his home, his hatred of *ad hoc* arrangements, and his horrified reaction to Priscilla's personal problems are all indicative of his obsessive desire for a planned, orderly, and disciplined life-style. Ironically, this uneventful, patterned existence is the reason he has been unable to produce the novel he wishes to write, and the chaotic events that disrupt his peace of mind are the catalyst for his writing *The Black Prince;* they are, in fact, the "object lesson in the foul contingency of life," which must be learned before he can become an artist. In this sense Bradley's development parallels that of Jake Donoghue in *Under the Net*, for Jake, who initially feels nausea when confronted with contingency, is able to make the transition from translator to creative writer only after accepting the accidental and unexplainable.

Robert Bernard Martin's statement that comic novels often announce themselves as such in the opening sentences is borne out in *The Black Prince*, for Bradley begins his novel by comically and characteristically agonizing over how best to begin his story, a nervous indecision that is later repeated when he attempts to decide at exactly what moment he fell in love with Julian Baffin. In fact, the comic tone is evident even earlier in P. Loxias's rather pompous foreword, in which his description of himself as a "clown or harlequin figure who parades before the curtain, then draws it solemnly back" undercuts the foreword's ostensibly serious tone and prepares the reader for the comedy to come (pp. ix–x).

Bradley's foreword intensifies this self-mocking attitude. Filled with words in quotation marks, a practice that recurs throughout the story and becomes an important characteristic of his style, the foreword reveals him as concerned with qualifying every word he uses, at times even stopping his narrative to define nouns and verbs for the reader. His introductory remarks also have the affected and pseudo-literary tone of Loxias's foreword. Bradley appears to want the reader to know from the very beginning that he views himself and his creation from a consciously ironic perspective, referring to his story as "this fable" and placing references to himself as a "hero" and "writer" in quotation marks. After describing himself as an "ageing Don Juan," he quickly notes that most of his conquests were fantasies, and his admission that he wishes to write a "sort of Seducer's Diary with metaphysical reflections" shows Bradley enjoying making jokes at his own expense. His characterization of his life as "sublimely dull, a great dull life" hardly seems an auspicious beginning for an autobiographical novel, nor does his confession that, although he had waited with anticipation for his retirement from the tax office, which would finally give him the time for artistic creation, he in fact discovered that "when I . . . could sit at my desk at home every morning and think any thoughts I pleased, I found I had no thoughts at all" (p. xvii). Although Bradley talks a great deal about creativity, he seems to equate it, ironically, with destruction: "In the years before, I worked steadily. That is, I wrote steadily and I destroyed steadily. I will not say how many pages I have destroyed, the number is immense. There was pride in this as well as sorrow" (p. xvi). The picture of Bradley that emerges in the foreword is that of an ironical man who talks about art but seems even more intent on keeping his gift, as he puts it, "pure," remaining silent in the face of possible mediocrity. His emphasis on his destroyed writings and the fact that he reveals he has published almost nothing place the reader in a curious position, for Bradley presents such a qualified and suspect portrait of himself as an artist that the reader tends to be skeptical about whether he actually *is* a novelist, even while in the process of reading his novel.

Bradley's description of himself as "conventional, nervous, puritanical, the slave of habit" is possible only because of his detachment; his objective depiction of himself is one aspect of his ironic sensibility that is responsible for the comic tone of the novel. In his postscript he calls himself an "ironical man," a description of his personality that has been obvious to the reader and is verified in the postscripts of the other characters. Rachel Baffin perceptively observes that the ironical style of the novel is Bradley's defense against laughter: "That BP was a man who hated being laughed at is pretty clear throughout the story. The rather pompous self-mocking style is a defense and a sort of meeting people half-way if they decide to laugh" (p. 354). Christian Evandale remarks that "he is quite witty sometimes in the book and makes things funny (sometimes he makes things funny which are not really)" (p. 344), while Francis Marloe remembers his "familiar self-conscious irony"(p. 350).

Rachel's description and explanation of the style of the novel are correct, for Bradley's fear of emotional scenes and involvements causes him to adopt a tone that both distances him from events and protects him from emotional damage by others. His fear of emotional invasion is evident in his remarks about his ex-wife; his reunion with Christian causes him to feel "that old fear of a misunderstanding which amounted to an invasion, a taking over of my thoughts" (p. 71) and later, discussing his marriage, he remembers that Christian had attempted "to invade and conquer me. . . . What saved me from Christian was art. My artist's soul rejected this massive invasion. (It was like an invasion of viruses)" (p. 156). The theme of invasion is present throughout *The Black Prince*. Many of the most comical scenes occur when Bradley, alone in his apartment and attempting to leave for the complete isolation of Patara, is suddenly besieged by several of the other characters. These incidents, although comically treated, show that Bradley's deepest fears of psychic invasion are coming true. When faced with the revelations and confessions of other individuals, his usual response is "I don't want to know," a statement that repeatedly reveals his desire to withdraw from the emotional demands of other people. His definition of a mental breakdown as "the semi-deliberate refusal to go on organizing one's life which is regarded with such tolerance in these days" is indicative of his fear and distaste for human misery and of his wish to distance himself, through precise, detached language, from the emotional turmoil that surrounds him (p. 52).

Bradley's belief that art saved him from the threat of an emotional takeover by his wife is directly related to his attitude about language, for he uses words and their potential for irony and abstraction to shield himself from too close a contact with reality. An art form composed of words is a defensive barrier that can protect him from emotional pain, a creation of an "elegant complexity" that moves farther and farther away from a direct confrontation with actual people and events. Speaking of his admittedly biased portrayal of Arnold Baffin, he says that "it is as if I were building a barrier against him composed of words, hiding myself behind a mound of words. We defend ourselves by descriptions and tame the world by generalizing. . . . Art is so often a barrier. . . . So art becomes not communication but mystification" (p. 58). The process of writing a novel is, for Bradley, a defensive act that enables him to "attain truth through irony," for the medium he uses, "this layered stuff of ironic sensibility," by its very nature obscures and distorts what it attempts to represent (p. 58). It is obvious that Bradley, who revels in the power of words to transform their subject because this alteration of reality can render it less frightening, exemplifies Wallace's belief that escape through artistic creation is a central theme of modern comic fiction: because language determines reality, says Wallace, the form of a novel is crucial, and the modern comic hero can best control the form of his reality by becoming an artist.[10] Wallace also observes that the writers of fictional autobiography frequently create their own history by revising the past to suit the needs of the present.[11] Rachel's interpretation of *The Black Prince* is based on this concept of artistic motivation, and though it is apparent that she is intent on protecting herself from the reader's disapprobation, it is also clear that Bradley's novel is an effort to capture and possess in aesthetic form the persons and events around him, to place them in a static, fixed position that he can manipulate for his own purposes. His statement in the postscript that *The Black Prince* is his "final possession" of Julian, "an embrace she can never now escape" (p. 339), clearly states this intention, although he does acknowledge that any kind of final possession of human beings through art is impossible: speaking to Julian, he says that "eternally you escape my embrace. Art cannot assimilate you nor thought digest you" (p. 341).

Bradley further refines his ideas about the function of language in the scene in which he "teaches" *Hamlet* to Julian. Shakespeare, he says, produced *Hamlet*, "a monument of words," because of his own lack of identity, and the play is about "the redemptive role of words in the lives of those without identity" (p. 166). Here Bradley gives the reader another insight into his reasons for writing *The Black Prince*, for he has earlier confessed that he has difficulty presenting himself to the reader in any definite way because he has always lacked any strong sense of his own identity. As a result, he is sympathetic with what he believes is Shakespeare's motive for writing *Hamlet:* that is, defining his own identity in an art work that is essentially comic:

> Shakespeare here makes the crisis of his own identity into the very central stuff of his art. He transmutes his private obsessions into a rhetoric so public that it can be mumbled by any child. He enacts the purification of speech, and yet also this is something

> comic, a sort of trick, like a huge pun, like a long almost pointless joke. Shakespeare cries out in agony, he writhes, he dances, he laughs, he shrieks, and he makes us laugh and shriek ourselves out of hell. Being is acting. We are tissues and tissues of different *personae* and yet we are nothing at all. What redeems us is that speech is ultimately divine. (P. 167)

Like his conception of Hamlet, Bradley believes that he himself is a man who is composed of words, who *is* words, and as a result the act of writing a novel is an act of self-definition: he is the product of the novel rather than simply its creator. His comment that in *Hamlet* Shakespeare is "speaking as few artists can speak, in the first person and yet at the pinnacle of artifice" is also applicable to *The Black Prince*, for in his novel Bradley seeks both to create an identity for himself and to use language as a way of defending and obscuring himself and his actions (p. 166).[12]

Bradley's opinion about the function of letters, which he describes as "a barrier, a reprieve, a charm against the world, an almost infallible method of acting at a distance" (p. 41), parallels his attitude toward his novel. He says he writes letters out of a "need for self-expression or self-defence," that they are a "magical warding-off movement" (p. 45), and a great deal of the comedy of *The Black Prince* results from his defensive use of language. He will choose to describe potentially dangerous or moving experiences in clinically detached language, will begin an extended passage of extremely abstract prose after being forced to undergo disturbing experiences, or will suddenly adopt a writing style that is self-consciously literary. These abrupt changes in tone are similar to the technique Murdoch uses in *An Accidental Man*, though in *The Black Prince* the changes are less dramatic and appear to function as emotional respites that enable Bradley to continue with the narrative.

People and situations that pose a threat to Bradley's emotional isolation and serenity are frequently treated in a detached, ironic manner which lessens their stature and importance for both the reader and narrator. The discrepancy between the events narrated, which include an attack of hysterics, a suicide attempt, a funeral, and Bradley's problem with impotence, and the manner in which they are treated, creates the ironic tone of much of the novel. Bradley speaks of his characterization of his sister as "crippled and diminished by my perception itself," a statement that can be applied to all the characters: Arnold, Rachel, Priscilla, and Christian are threatening figures whom Bradley belittles through comically unattractive portraits. Arnold is described as having a particularly "greasy" appearance that Bradley calls his "drenched albino aspect" and later is described more ridiculously as having the look of a "fanatical gunman." Rachel's physical appearance, like Priscilla's, gets progressively more inelegant during the course of the novel. The reader first sees her after she has been beaten up by Arnold, sporting swollen eyes, lips, and tangled hair; a later description is equally unflattering:

> She was wearing a sleeveless, cream-coloured dress. The back was unhooked, the zip not fully up, revealing lumpy vertebrae covered with reddish down. A satiny shoulder strap, not clean, had flopped down over the vaccination mark on her plump pallid arm. The armholes of the dress cut into the bulging flesh of the shoulder. (Pp. 143–44)

Bradley repeatedly focuses on Rachel's unattractive characteristics because she is a potentially disturbing force, for her sexual designs on him continuously place him in defensive and awkward positions that he chooses to treat comically. Their first embrace is described in terms more funereal than erotic: "She had wound her arm underneath my arm and rather awkwardly taken hold of my hand. So two corpses might ineptly greet each other on resurrection day" (p. 92), and his choice of sepulchral imagery to characterize Rachel continues until the end of the novel, when he remarks that "seeing Rachel there in the flat was like a bad trip in a time machine. There was a memory-odour like a smell of decay. . . . It was as if my mother had visited me in her cerements" (p. 306). When Rachel attempts to seduce Bradley, the scene's tone is unequivocally unerotic, partially due to the molluscous quality of her kisses: "Her wet mouth travelled across my cheek and settled upon my mouth, like the celestial snail closing the great gate" (p. 112). Bradley's efforts to reduce Rachel and her sexual demands to absurdity through the use of comically grotesque language are almost always successful, and they reveal a detachment from sexual activity in general and Rachel in particular which is most evident in the scene in which he is unable to make love to her:

> To lie fully clothed, with one's shoes on, beside a panting naked woman is not perhaps very gentlemanly. I raised myself on one elbow so that I could see her face. I did not want to be submerged by this warm gale. . . . I felt excited, stunned, but this was not quite desire. I seemed to be outside, seeing myself as in a picture, a fully dressed elderly man in a dark suit and a blue tie lying beside a pink naked pear-shaped lady. (Pp. 128–29)

Priscilla and Christian are dealt with in a similar fashion, though Priscilla's problems are treated with a degree of sympathy and pathos, while Christian, like Francis, remains a completely comic character. Priscilla, like Rachel, is described as resembling a corpse and also as having a great deal of "mottled flesh," which perpetually bulges through holes in clothing. Although Christian has less weight than the other two women, Bradley is equally repulsed by her physicality, saying that she has a face like a "grotesque ancient mask"; later, when she asks Bradley to kiss her, her face is described as looking "older, more animal-like and absurd, her features all squashed up and rubbery" (p. 193). In a review of *The Black Prince* Kennedy Fraser says that Murdoch often "surveys her characters' progress through the grubbier aspects of this jumble with uncharitable glee."[13] Her narrator, who does indeed revel in his comically grotesque descriptions of characters, does this so that he can bring them under his imaginative control and limit their power to affect him. It has been seen earlier that enjoyment of other people's problems and discomfitures is a recurrent theme in Murdoch's fiction, and she observes in *The Sacred and Profane Love Machine* that irony is the technique the author must use to express the "glee" he feels about what he is expressing: "An author's irony often conceals his glee. This concealment is possibly the chief function of irony."[14] Irony, the indirect method that enables a writer to express his enjoyment of the horror around him, allows the writer, through aesthetic manipulation, to exert a degree of control over the elements of his narrative. Bradley makes extensive use of ironical and comical language to reveal both his delight in his narrative and his need to control his subject matter.

Events as well as people cause Bradley to adopt a critical stance that is frequently humorous in light of the emotional explosions that are occurring around him. He prefers to take refuge in irony and abstraction after being forced to participate in upsetting events; after the "invasions" by other characters, he will often begin a narrative section set off from the dramatic scenes composed entirely of his personal definitions and explanations of earlier events, making generalized pronouncements about the concepts involved in a pompous, magisterial tone comically at variance with the events being narrated. Priscilla's first suicide attempt, rendered in a frenetic and farcical manner, culminates in Bradley's dashing from his flat in horror after learning that Arnold has left with his ex-wife. This scene is immediately followed by an extended philosophical meditation on art and truth addressed to P. Loxias. Bradley says that speaking directly to Loxias in the novel is "a kind of relief, it eases some pressure upon the heart and upon the intelligence"; in reality, however, it enables Bradley to withdraw behind the protective barrier of language from the painful fact that his sister has tried to kill herself and from the specter of Arnold's possible friendship with Christian (p. 56). When another incursion into the flat occurs soon after, with Hartbourne, Priscilla, Francis, Arnold, and Christian vying for Bradley's attention, he again leaves his home in an effort to avoid becoming involved with what is happening, instead launching into a discussion of marriage:

> Marriage is a curious institution, as I have already remarked. I cannot quite see how it can be possible. People who boast of happy marriages are, I submit, usually self-deceivers, if not actually liars. The human soul is not framed for continued proximity, and the result of this enforced neighbourhood is often an appal-

> ling loneliness for which the rules of the game forbid assuagement. There is nothing like the bootless solitude of those who are caged together. Those outside the cage can, to their own taste, satisfy their need for society by more or less organized dashes in the direction of other human beings. But the unit of two can scarcely communicate with others, and is fortunate, as the years go by, if it can communicate within itself. (P. 67)

This precise verbal dissection of marriage is necessary before Bradley can go on to discuss his relationship with Christian. When he does begin to describe their marriage, he nevertheless feels a need to qualify his choice of words with a liberal use of quotation marks, a characteristic of his style that signals an uneasiness with his subject matter. Bradley says that he goes to see Christian to "dilute" the power of her meeting with Arnold, and his ironically philosophical speculations about marriage are an attempt to lessen the pain caused by the memory of their relationship. On the way to Patara Julian tells Bradley, who is trying to avoid a total involvement in their relationship by manufacturing textbook definitions about the particular quality of their love, that abstract language is one form of lying. Julian later asks, "Well, why do you say these sort of abstract things that you don't mean?"; his reply, "I'm just instinctively protecting myself," reveals his need to intellectualize his emotions in order to maintain an emotional distance from potentially distressing situations (p. 274).

Priscilla's attack of hysterics, described in a coldly detached manner that removes the reader from her misery, is another example of Bradley's efforts to retain a degree of control over what is happening around him by intellectualizing his responses. Before actually discussing his sister, he goes through a short analysis of hysterics which reveals his talent for using precise, objective language to describe emotionally wrenching events:

> Priscilla suddenly started to scream quietly. "Scream quietly" may sound like an oxymoron, but I mean to indicate the curiously controlled rhythmic screaming which goes with a certain kind of hysterics. Hysterics is terrifying because of its willed and yet not

> willed quality. It has the frightfulness of a deliberate assault on the spectators, yet it is also, with its apparently unstoppable rhythm, like the setting-going of a machine. It is no use asking someone in hysterics to "control themselves." By "choosing" to become hysterical they have put themselves beyond ordinary communication. Priscilla, now sitting upright in bed, gave a gasping "Uuuh!" then a screamed "Aaah!" ending in a sort of bubbling sob, then the gasp again and the scream and so on. (P. 189)

Bradley's horror of the lack of organization and control that mental illness reflects has already been mentioned, and he predictably takes cover in clinically detached language to describe his sister's attack of hysterics, a dramatic example of an event he is poorly equipped to handle. Julian's leap from the moving automobile is treated in much the same manner; instead of immediately revealing what has happened to her, Bradley indulges in a soliloquy reminiscent of Hamlet's "What a piece of work is a man!":

> Oh the poor frailty of the human form, its egg-shell vulnerability! How can this precarious crushable machine of flesh and bones and blood survive on this planet of hard surfaces and relentless murderous gravity? I had felt the crash and crunch of her body on the road. (P. 265)

Bradley, like Hamlet, prefers to withdraw behind the protective barrier of words rather than immediately to grasp and act upon the situation that confronts him. His first attempt to make love to Julian is ironically prefaced by references to "To His Coy Mistress"; escaping into literary and historical references comically underscores his personal failure and protects his ego.

It is not unusual for Bradley to deal with sexual matters in this manner, and, in fact, any kind of sexual confrontation usually results in a humorously abstract philosophical meditation. One of his encounters with Rachel is the immediate cause for the following pronouncement on sex, another example of Bradley's neutralization of a disturbing subject by assuming a stance of ironic detachment:

> It is customary in this age to attribute a comprehensive and quite unanalysed causality to the "sexual urges." These obscure forces, sometimes thought of as particular historical springs, sometimes as more general and universal destinies, are credited with the power to make of us delinquents, neurotics, lunatics, fanatics, martyrs, heroes, saints, or more exceptionally, integrated fathers, fulfilled mothers, placid human animals, and the like. . . . I am myself no sort of Freudian and I feel it important at this stage of my "exploration" or "apologia," or whatever this malformed treatise may be said to be, to make this clear beyond the possibility of misunderstanding. I abominate such half-baked tosh. My own sense of the "beyond," which heaven forbid anyone should confuse with anything "scientific," is quite other. (P. 115)

The fact that Bradley disavows sex as an important force in the lives of human beings is extremely ironic in light of the metamorphosis that occurs after his realization of his love for Julian; sex is then exaltedly described as "the great connective principle whereby we overcome duality, the force which made separateness as an aspect of oneness at some moment of bliss in the mind of God" (p. 176). What Bradley characterizes as "half-baked tosh" later becomes what he calls the "Black Eros," the force that is the catalyst for *The Black Prince*. However, because of his need to remain isolated from the physical and emotional demands of sexual activity, his description of an erection as "the anti-gravitational aspiration of the male organ, one of the oddest and most unnerving things in nature" (pp. 133–34) has a tone of detached clinical wonder about his own body, a tone that is repeated in his comical description of the act of vomiting:

> Vomiting is a curious experience, entirely *sui generis*. It is involuntary in a peculiarly shocking way, the body suddenly doing something very unusual with great promptness and decision. One cannot argue. One is *seized*. And the fact that one's vomit moves with such a remarkable drive contrary to the force of gravity adds to the sense of being taken and shaken by some alien power. I am told that there are people who enjoy vomiting, and although I do not share their taste I can, I think, faintly imagine it. There is a certain sense of achievement. And if one does not fight against the

stomach's decree there is perhaps some satisfaction in being its helpless vehicle. (P. 221)

Bradley's sense of detachment from his physical being, an attitude that parallels his need to intellectualize his emotions by means of philosophical speculation, makes this sort of analytical description possible and reveals his fear of losing control both of his bodily functions and of his emotional stability. The resulting efforts to maintain a rational control through verbalization of experiences and emotions that are often intrinsically ungovernable illustrate Kerr's belief that sex is amusing because it transforms man into an "ardent anarchist."

The subtitle of Bradley's novel, *A Celebration of Love*, reflects the central event of the novel, his sudden passion for Julian Baffin and its results. Just as Murdoch believes that a comic treatment of any event in no way diminishes its importance and seriousness, Bradley's short-lived affair with the daughter of his best friend is presented in both a serious and comic light. Bradley, who has earlier painted devastating portraits of the other characters, allows himself to metamorphose into a buffoon-figure, and seems to delight in revealing himself behaving foolishly and often idiotically over a woman thirty-eight years his junior. His immediate reaction to the situation is to lie face down on a rug for hours, meditating on the metaphysics of love. After the regretful observation that literature usually neglects to describe falling in love properly, he attempts to rectify this failure by writing his own self-consciously literary description of the process, calling it a "predestined collision" that "had not only just happened, it had happened aeons ago, it was of the stuff of the original formation of earth and sky. When God said, 'Let there be light,' this love was made. It had no history" (p. 172). The comically exaggerated tone of this description recurs throughout his affair, while at the same time the reader is convinced of the reality and importance of his emotion. Bradley describes his new love-sick personality with the same glee that he earlier used to depict the faults of the other characters; his description of *Hamlet* as a "wild act of audacity, a self-purging, a complete self-castigation" is applicable to the self-mocking presentation of himself in the second half of the novel (p. 166). Some of the most humorous scenes occur when the previously introverted, dour Bradley is transformed into a warm, outgoing individual who delights in socializing with persons he has earlier disliked or ignored: his conversations with Rachel and later with Roger and Marigold are examples. The description of a later phase of his love is ridiculously exaggerated:

> I could not stand still but wandered distractedly and rapidly around the flat, rubbing against the furniture as a tiger in a cage endlessly brushes against its bars. I had ceased groaning and was now *hissing*. I tried to compose a few thoughts about the future. Should I kill myself? Should I go at once to Patara and barricade myself in and blow my mind with alcohol? Run, run, run. (P. 208)

The comic high point of the love affair occurs at the performance of *Rosenkavalier*, where Bradley suddenly begins weeping during the music, then moans, and finally dashes from the theater in order to vomit, hardly a romantic beginning for the exalted passion he has described earlier. The discrepancy between Bradley's aesthetic and philosophical pronouncements and the reality of human involvement is both absurd and comical.

Even Bradley's trial and conviction for a murder he has not committed are treated in a darkly comic manner, and he maintains his detached, ironic stance throughout the description of the court trial. He chooses to end the novel proper before his imprisonment, briefly and comically summarizing the trial in the postscript. Bradley characteristically treats his trial, conviction, and resulting life imprisonment as an artistic experience, once again "taking refuge in irony" to protect himself from the emotional implications of what has occurred. His statement that "some newspapers said I seemed to enjoy my trial. I did not enjoy it, but I experienced it very intently and fully," is telling, for Bradley describes the entire experience as if he were an actor playing the leading role in a comic drama, discussing and analyzing his role offstage (p. 333).

The description of the trial begins, typically, with a paragraph discussing the inability of human beings to understand the circumstances of their lives, a philosophical preface that by now clearly signals to the reader that Bradley is about to deal with potentially disturbing events. The fact that he has chosen to view the trial aesthetically is obvious from his statement that "it was like going through a glass and finding oneself inside a picture by Goya" (pp. 331–32). Art, which has protected Bradley so often in the novel, does not fail him now; he is able to describe Rachel's final revenge on Arnold and himself as "a sort of perfection" as she settles into "her final dreadful role." He even mentions that he considered "assuming" Arnold's death by a false confession as an "aesthetic possibility": "If I *had* killed him there would have been a certain beauty in it. And to an ironical man what could be prettier than to have the aesthetic satisfaction of having 'committed' murder, without actually having had to commit it?", noting that this "picturesque explanation" had some force because of the "appeal of the picturesqueness to my literary mind" (p. 337). Bradley had hinted earlier that he felt he must go through some sort of "ordeal" before he could become an artist, and, although the reader at first believes that his affair with Julian Baffin is this experience, Bradley reveals in his postscript that the trial is actually the event he has been awaiting:

> I had been forcibly presented with a new mode of being and I was anxious to explore it. I had been confronted (at last) with a sizeable *ordeal* labelled with my name. This was not something to be wasted. I had never felt more alert and alive in my life, and from the vantage point of my new consciousness I looked upon what I had been: a timid incomplete resentful man. (P. 333)

On trial for murder, Bradley sounds as if he is instead experiencing an emotional rebirth, and he remains more a witness than a participant in the events of the trial, viewing it almost without exception from a comic perspective.

Bradley then begins a comical description of the actual proceedings of the trial, shouting at Hartbourne—a member of the "insanity lobby," who is attempting to convince the jury that he is mad—that "that cock won't fight, old man!" (p. 334). Hartbourne's evidence for this opinion, that Bradley frequently canceled appointments and was moody, eccentric, and absent-minded, is obviously slim, and Bradley ironically applauds the prosecution counsel's objection "But he *is* a writer!" to Hartbourne's statement that Bradley "imagined" himself a writer (p. 334). Francis makes a predictably poor showing at the trial and succeeds only in convincing the jury that Bradley murdered Arnold in a fit of homosexual jealousy. Christian, who finds the trial almost as enjoyable as Priscilla's funeral, dresses in fashionable clothing to help advertise her soon-to-be-opened *haute couture* shop, and the guilty Rachel behaves with a "modest simplicity" and "an air of gentle quiet exact truthfulness" that moves even Bradley to a "sort of sigh of reverent appreciation" (p. 336). Bradley's attitude toward the trial clearly reveals that he is reveling in its artistic dimension as a comic drama with carefully assigned roles for each participant.

Bradley's description of himself at the trial has another aspect that reflects the structure of ironic comedy: he makes it obvious that he views himself as a scapegoat figure, as one who is set up to represent the stereotype of a murderer and the dark forces this kind of figure embodies, and is consequently banished:

> In a purely technical sense I was condemned for having murdered Arnold. (The jury were out of the room for less than half an hour. Counsel did not even bother to leave their seats.) In a more extended sense, and this too provided fruit for meditation, I was condemned for being a certain awful kind of person. I aroused horror and aversion in the bosom of the judge and in the bosoms of the honest citizens of the jury and the sturdy watchdogs of the press. I was heartily hated. In sentencing me to life imprisonment the judge gave general satisfaction. (Pp. 336–37)

At this point in the narrative Bradley has played all four of the major roles of comedy, functioning as *eiron*, buffoon, *pharmakos*, and "possessed artist," and viewing himself with ironic detachment in each role. He plays the part of the frenzied writer throughout *The Black Prince*, for he envisages himself as possessed by the demands of a god he cannot see or understand, but who is responsible for both his experiences and the novel that results. Sypher says that "the fool can also be the seer, the prophet, the 'possessed,' since the madness of the fool is oracular, sibylline, delphic," and Bradley certainly sees himself as one who is privileged to have arcane knowledge and to be speaking hidden truths.[15] It is no accident that his editor's name, Loxias, is one of the names of Apollo meaning "crooked" or "ambiguous," and that one of his oracles was at Patara.[16]

The presence of postscripts by Rachel, Francis, Julian, Christian, and P. Loxias creates a further comic dimension to the novel. In *An Accidental Man* Murdoch uses chapters consisting solely of dialogue or letters to expand the fictional boundaries of the narrative, creating a comic perspective that results from the ever-widening framework of the novel. She achieves a similar kind of narrative expansion in *The Black Prince* by having four of the participants analyze and comment on the story, forcing the reader to move outside Bradley's consciousness and view his novel simply as one version of the events narrated. This technique, which both calls into question the truthfulness of his story and validates his observations and conclusions, for the most part reveals the characters to be as foolish, self-centered, and comical as he has depicted them.

Rachel's postscript is her final revenge on Bradley, and her description of him as a rather pitiful buffoon-figure parallels his unflattering characterization of her in *The Black Prince*. She strips him of dignity and denies him many of the characteristics he has taken such pains to convince the reader he possesses:

> In reality he was a person quite without dignity. His appearance was absurd. And no one could possibly have taken him for being younger than his age. He was a stiff, awkward man, very timid and shy, and yet at the same time he could be quite pushing. He was often, to put it bluntly, rather a bore. The pretence of being

> an artist was psychologically necessary to him. I am told this is so with a lot of unsuccessful people. (P. 354)

Rachel's postscript places the reader in the curious position of believing many of her insights into Bradley's personality that totally contradict his presentation of himself, while at the same time continuing to accept his version of the story. She reduces Bradley to a "figure of fun" and intimates that he killed her husband simply to make people stop laughing at him; Julian, she says, regarded him merely as a "funny uncle" and the "family pussycat." The novel itself she dismisses as a fantasy and a "farrago of lies," concluding that the ultimate cause of all of the events was Bradley's passion for her. Christian emerges as the self-centered and self-satisfied character Bradley presented in the novel, while Francis Marloe's postscript, a comically distorted Freudian interpretation of *The Black Prince* based on his belief in Bradley's latent homosexuality, reads like a parody of psychological literary criticism. Julian's postscript reveals her to be a pompous and self-conscious young woman who, as P. Loxias notes in his final summation of the story, imitates Bradley's writing style while denying his influence.

Loxias, who says that he has decided against writing a long analysis of his own because the novel speaks for itself, does proceed to discuss Bradley's work and the four postscripts that precede his. By mentioning the possibility of another reading of the novel, Loxias hints at the work's potential to continue on and on, and the reader can easily imagine the characters taking issue with his opinions and writing further interpretations and denials. Murdoch suggests here, as in *An Accidental Man*, the novel's ability to continue to expand, encompassing more and more reality, and she accomplishes this by allowing other characters to surface as independent entities, released from the constraint of Bradley's consciousness. Langer has said that the movement of comedy is always expansive, that it assumes that "more life, more destiny" continue after the end of the story, and Murdoch indeed makes use of this characteristic of comedy to structure the narrative of *The Black Prince*.

The postscripts, humorous in themselves, present various comic perspectives on the story and prove Bradley's statement that "every man is tiny and comic to his neighbor" (p. 339).

The Black Prince is, in a sense, a novel about laughter and how people perceive others as comic. Bradley belittles the characters in his narrative and is in turn mocked by the postscript writers. The laughter that rings throughout the novel usually functions to ridicule and degrade other people: Christian and Arnold collapse with laughter at almost everything that happens; Rachel tells Bradley that she and Arnold have laughed both at him and at his passion for Julian; and Francis warns Bradley that Julian's reaction to his confession of love will probably be laughter. Bradley's novel is his attempt to portray the people around him as ridiculously comic figures and simultaneously to reveal himself as a fool. Rachel's statement that the events of the novel, for Bradley, have been a "voyage into the absurd" is correct, and Bradley's description of *Hamlet* as a "long almost pointless joke" can also be applied to *The Black Prince*, for Murdoch, who has expressed her agreement with the Zen concept of human life as a "sort of wild joke," creates a narrator whose vision is essentially comic and who is in turn treated as a comic figure by the other characters. June Sturrock's belief that the novel is flawed by the "over-activity" of Murdoch's comic gifts fails to take into consideration Murdoch's (and Bradley Pearson's) conception of both human life and the novel form itself as inherently comic.[17] P. Loxias, speaking for Murdoch in his postscript, says that "all human beings are figures of fun. Art celebrates this," and further remarks that "the work of art laughs last" (pp. 364–65). *The Black Prince*, a novel about a comic apprehension of human beings and their misguided actions, reflects its subject matter in both its comic structure and its tone.

5

The Director as *Alazon* in *The Sea, The Sea*

At the first glance *The Sea, The Sea* appears to be an alternate version of *The Black Prince.* What, Murdoch seems to be asking, might have happened had Bradley Pearson been able to escape to his seaside retreat and begun to write his novel there? Charles Arrowby, the narrator of *The Sea, The Sea,* has several characteristics in common with Bradley: extreme self-consciousness about the form his novel is to take—"diary," "memoir," "philosophical journal," or "novelistic memoir"? Also, at sixty he is the fussy, eccentric, soon-to-be-elderly bachelor who frequently appears in Murdoch's fiction. Unlike Bradley Pearson, however, he is an eminently successful theatrical director who has also had a career as an actor and playwright and is accustomed to manipulating the people around him both on and offstage. Charles, who makes little effort to hide his self-love, admits that he has retired from the theater and come to the sea "to repent of egoism," and he takes obvious satisfaction in recounting his past reputation in the theater as a tartar. His novel, a chronicle of the delusions and errors in judgment that result from his egotism, for the most part lacks the self-mocking, ironically detached tone of Bradley Pearson's narrative. Just as Bradley resembles the *eiron* figure in comedy, Charles is an *alazon* character, whom Wallace describes as an impostor or fool who pretends to be more than he really is. Wallace believes that the modern comic hero is derived from the *alazon* archetype and that it is more typical for this character to remain deluded until the end of the story rather than being converted to the reason and order that society represents. The comedy arises from the discrepancy between the character's interpretation of his situation and the reader's perception of it, and the comic potential of unconscious self-exposure is even greater when the hero narrates his own fiction.[1] Wallace also maintains that the modern comic hero is a fusion of the *eiron* and *alazon* archetypes: like the *alazon*, the hero usually fails to learn more about himself by the end of the story, but resembles the *eiron* in that he frequently is an artist who is intent on creating an imaginative world for himself.[2] Charles Arrowby, who views himself as a Prospero-like magician-artist, gradually reveals to the reader his incorrect evaluations of both himself and others, and much of the novel's comedy is dependent upon the ironic discrepancy between Charles's interpretation of events and the reader's own conclusions. Too egotistical and self-involved to be capable of Bradley Pearson's self-mocking narrative style, Charles instead embarks at the age of sixty on a romantic quest for a woman he loved forty years earlier, only at rare moments acknowledging that his "quest" may have a humorous dimension.

In *An Accidental Man* and *The Black Prince* Murdoch makes use of the plot structures of traditional comedy, ironic comedy, and the ironic mode; in *The Sea, The Sea* she moves toward the genre of romantic comedy in Frye's scheme and manipulates both the structure and characters of the romantic mode for ironic purposes. In *The Sea, The Sea* Murdoch runs the gamut of the comic mode, combining characteristics of fourth-, fifth-, and sixth-phase comedy, phases that, because they often contain events and persons that are mysterious and unrealistic, allow her to include occult phenomena which add a magical dimension to the novel. The structure of fourth-phase comedy, which begins to move away from the world of experience into an ideal world of innocence and romance, frequently includes a ritual assault on a central female figure and/or a rejuvenation of an impotent king. Frye calls this idyllic society the "green world" and believes it analogous to "the dream world that we create out of our own desires."[3] In *The Sea, The Sea* this romantically innocent world is ostensibly represented by Charles's seaside retreat, where he hopes to abandon the complexities of the past for what he calls "happy and innocent reflections." Although he believes he is leaving the corrupt world of the London theater behind him, in reality the innocent idealism he is seeking exists only in the mythical past he has created for himself. In search of his lost innocence, his frenzied pursuit of Mary Hartley Fitch is the result of his desire to recapture an idealized memory of the chastity and purity of an adolescent relationship. As usual, however, Murdoch inverts typical comic structures for comic effect, for Charles never rediscovers his lost innocence, and his emotional impotence is not healed by his assault on Hartley's life. In fact, he merely brings the sophisticated, complicated world of the West End to his "retreat," and by the end of the novel he has returned to London and the worldliness it represents. The "dream world" that symbolizes a more idealized existence is present in Charles's mind only, and his attempt to force real events into a falsely romantic shape and form has both comical and disastrous results. The word *dream*, which occurs many times in reference to his passion for Hartley, leads several characters to try to convince him that she is only a "dream figure," and at one point even the uncommunicative Hartley makes an effort to persuade Charles that their love is a "dream" that does not belong in the real world; only much later, when he refers to his novel as "my own dream text," does he finally admit the truth of her statement.

The conclusion of fifth-phase comedy, less festive and more pensive than that of the fourth phase, often depends upon the audience's perspective rather than upon the actual outcome of the plot. In this kind of comedy, which can contain a tragic action within itself and usually posits an upper world of order and a lower world of confusion and chaos, the reader views the action from the vantage point of the "upper world" and looks down upon the characters as representative of typical, generic human behavior; the lower, chaotic world is sometimes symbolized by the sea, from which the cast or an individual member must be saved.[4] In *The Sea, The Sea* the sea does indeed function as a symbol of what is chaotic and ungovernable in human life, and the point of ritual death, for Charles, occurs when he is pushed into the sea and is magically rescued by James. Like many of Murdoch's novels, *The Sea, The Sea* contains tragedy: Titus, the scapegoat figure, is drowned; James dies; and Charles loses Hartley for the second time. Because, however, the reader begins to perceive a discrepancy between Charles's interpretation of events and what the reader believes to be true, the tragedy is tempered; for although Titus's death remains tragic, Hartley's defection and the death of James are not, and as a result the reader has the sensation of viewing the action of the book from the more knowledgeable perspective that Frye speaks of. The novel's postscript also mitigates the more serious tone of the novel proper by calling into question the truthfulness and sincerity of the narrator's presentation of events.

Several elements of comedy in its sixth and most romantic phase are also to be found in *The Sea, The Sea*, for comedy in this phase has a mystical quality that is frequently dependent upon the presence of the occult and the marvelous. Although this category consists of ghost stories, thrillers, and Gothic romances, it can also include literature of a more sophisticated type that depicts some kind of "imaginative withdrawal" from everyday existence.[5] In *The Sea, The Sea*, Murdoch's most magical book, she gives her love of the occult a nearly free rein while keeping the novel grounded in a realistic presentation of the subject matter. Speaking of James's magical powers in the novel, Margaret Drabble notes that "Quasi-naturalistic suggestions are offered for these powers, but the questions remain open."[6] Although Murdoch does not want what Frye terms an "uncritical surrender" to the mysterious events that occur, she refuses to differentiate what may be "real" from what may be Charles's hallucinations because she wants to force the reader to accept the possibility of the strange and marvelous. Rational explanations are given for the broken vase and mirror, and the sea monster can be explained either by an LSD flashback or a psychological projection, but the mysterious face at the window and James's descent into Minn's Cauldron are never accounted for rationally. What Frye calls an "imaginative withdrawal" occurs, for Charles, on two levels: he withdraws from the real world to construct his own imaginative drama, and, in the process, enters a new world of occult phenomena, symbolized by his strange new house, which he describes as "a sensitized plate which intermittently registered things which had happened in the past—or, it now occurred to me for the first time, were going to happen in the future."[7]

This is not the first time Murdoch has fused occult phenomena and comedy. In an article on Murdoch's early novels, Frank Baldanza comments on her ability to combine the supernatural and the comic, saying that "the extraordinary richness of character and incident in these novels is managed by an intelligence and a feeling for comedy that work together with an unusual skill at evoking a sense of nearly supernatural mystery and *bizarrerie*." Baldanza, who uses Martin Lynch-Gibbon's meeting with Honor Klein at the Liverpool Street Station in *A Severed Head* as an example of Murdoch's talent for combining mystery and comedy, nevertheless believes that "the sense of mystery in these novels is not fundamentally supernatural since it is insistently based on the characters' views of one another."[8] In a 1968 interview with W. K. Rose, Murdoch acknowledged her belief in a kind of demonology based on our perceptions of one another:

> This notion of the intrusion of demons—well, I feel this is something that happens in life. Not necessarily that people really are demons but that they play the role of demons for other people. . . . People are often looking for a god or ready to cast somebody in the role of a demon.[9]

However, in her more recent novels Murdoch shows an increased interest in mysticism, particularly Eastern religion and philosophy, and she would appear to be moving closer to a belief in the "fundamentally supernatural" than in her early work. In *The Sea, The Sea* she uses the occult in such a way that the mysterious events cannot be explained merely through one character's "casting" another in the role of supernatural being:

James's supernatural powers, for example, are not simply the product of Charles's imagination.

In *An Accidental Man* and *The Black Prince* Murdoch manipulates the structures of typical and ironic comedy, and in *The Sea, The Sea* she rearranges several elements of the romantic mode to achieve comic effects. The quest, usually the central event of the romance, appears in this novel in the form of Charles's pursuit of Hartley, what he ironically calls at one point his "Quest of the Bearded Lady." According to Frye, the reward of the quest is frequently a bride, but the hero must go through a series of adventures or conflicts to win her; the most important form of the quest-romance is the dragon-killing theme, in which a kingdom ruled by a helpless old king is pillaged by a sea monster which the hero must kill in order to win the bride and restore the waste land to fertility.[10] Charles, who refers to himself as a "king" several times in the narrative and is called the "king of shadows" by several of the other characters, is troubled by his repeated sightings of a sea serpent, a monster that represents his jealousy and his need to possess and dominate those around him. Significantly, he uses the same images he employed to describe his first vision of the sea monster to describe his hatred and jealousy of Hartley's husband, Ben:

> and as the violent feelings became calmer another emotion, darker, deeper, came slowly up from below. Or rather there were two emotions closely, blackly, coiled together. . . . The other emotion which now, closely embraced with this one, rose dark and gleaming to the surface was this: a kind of frightful glee. (P. 152)

At the conclusion of the novel Charles admits that he has let loose his own "demons," and specifically mentions the "sea serpent of jealousy." Peregrine Arbelow speaks of jealousy in the same terms, calling Charles, who had earlier taken his wife from him, a "monster in his mind" and says that his attempted murder "killed the monster" for him. Unable to control his jealousy, Charles, who fails to win his "bride," in this instance a sixty-year-old former girl friend who has been married to another man for forty years, is unable to restore his personal wasteland, and his life remains as emotionally empty as it was when the story began.

In *The Sea, The Sea* Charles plays the part of two of the characters of romance, both that of the fisher king in need of rejuvenation and, ironically, that of the vigorous, youthful hero who quests for the bride. He remarks several times that he wishes to marry Hartley so that he can regain the ordinary world of innocence and human commitment that he feels he has missed, and though he says he wants to "recreate" Hartley for his own purposes, he also believes that she can restore the past for him. Several characters in the novel correspond to figures that frequently appear in the typical quest-romance and act, in Frye's terms, as the "antagonists" of the quest, sinister characters such as ogres, witches, and magicians, who attempt to prevent the hero from achieving his object. Charles tries to cast Ben in the role of murderous tyrant holding his wife captive at Nibletts, while Rosina, whose next film role will be the part of Calypso in Fritzie Eitel's *Odyssesy*, functions as the "evil witch" of the story. The film star, whose physical beauty is marred by a cast in one eye, smashes vases, mirrors, and finally the windshield of her ex-husband's car, and tears Charles with her fingernails; she is indeed a kind of prophetic sorceress, for her insights into Charles's shortcomings are usually correct, and her remarks about Titus prove to be prophetic. James and Gilbert, on the other hand, correspond to those characters in romance who, as friends of the hero, aid him in the quest's completion. James represents the character who is the counterpart to the benevolent *eiron* of comedy, frequently a wise old man or magician who has a decisive effect on the action.[11] Although the reader is never sure to what extent he is manipulating events, James, the true magician in the novel, saves Charles's life, prevents him from possibly attempting to murder Ben, and may have "drawn" Titus to Shruff End through the power of his mind. Gilbert has more in common with the buffoon of typical comedy, excelling in his role as servant and enjoying, as does Francis Marloe in *The Black Prince*, cooking, cleaning, and serving his "master"; appropriately, Gilbert later becomes the star of a television comedy series. *The Sea, The Sea*, like the typical quest-romance, also contains several "precious objects": the pink stone Charles gives Hartley and the brown stone James takes from Shruff End are later considered by Charles to have almost magical properties. Though the novel is not an extended parody of the romantic mode, Murdoch does make use of the structure and characters of romance for ironic effects.

Murdoch has a basic distrust of individuals who confuse life and art, who attempt to impose an aesthetic structure upon real-life people and events. Hannah Crean-Smith's tragic ending in *The Unicorn* and Rupert Foster's death in *A Fairly Honourable Defeat* result from the tendency of other characters to view them as religious or aesthetic symbols, just as Mischa Fox in *The Flight from the Enchanter* enjoys manipulating the lives of others for aesthetic effects. Murdoch believes that "ordinary life is not dramatic . . . . ordinary life doesn't have shape"; it is too "jumbled" and "messy," to use two of her favorite adjectives, to have the tight aesthetic structure that characterizes art, particularly dramatic art. As a result, individuals who endeavor to mold reality into artistic form are committing a serious moral error that often has tragic consequences.[12] Murdoch is even uneasy about the fact that the artist must impose form upon the work of art:

> I think art's a kind of temptation in a way. I mean, art is a harmless activity, but it represents a sort of temptation, a temptation to impose form where perhaps it isn't always appropriate. . . . Morality has to do with not imposing form, except appropriately and cautiously and carefully and with attention to appropriate detail, and I think that truth is very fundamental here. Art can subtly tamper with truth to a great degree because art is enjoyment. People persist in being artists against every possible discouragement and disappointment, because it's a marvelous activity, a gratification of the ego, and a free, omnipotent imposition of form; unless this is constantly being, as it were, pulled at by the value of truth, the artwork itself may not be as good and the artist may be simply using art as a form of self-indulgence. So I think in

> art itself there is this conflict between the form maker and the truthful, formless figure. This happens in art as well as in life.[13]

Poetry and the theater, she believes, are the genres that, because they lack fiction's capacity for representing the formless nature of reality, tend to have a better-defined dramatic shape. Charles Arrowby, a recently retired theatrical director whose friends have correctly predicted that he will be unable to leave the stage behind him, mistakenly tries to "direct" life offstage because he has been accustomed to the artificiality and dramatic structure of the theater. In *The Sea, The Sea* Murdoch's concern with people who blur the distinctions between life and art takes the form of the close real-life relationships her actor-characters have with their theatrical roles: Rosina's and Gilbert's acting roles parallel their real personalities, while Peregrine, who tries to murder Charles, plays the part of a villain on his television series.

Just as Bradley Pearson creates a novel as a result of his need to hide behind words, Charles takes this aesthetic view of life one step farther, constructing a drama out of the lives of real people. He tells the reader that his last great acting role was as Prospero in *The Tempest*, and he believes that he has a great deal in common with Shakespeare's magician, mentioning that the critics remarked on the almost childish delight in the technical trickery of the theater that characterized his productions. Even though he states in the early pages of his story that "now I shall abjure magic and become a hermit," in reality he is about to begin the direction of his final drama (p. 2). Several characters in the novel consider him to be a kind of Prospero-like magician figure: Lizzie Scherer calls him a "rapacious magician"; Rosina angrily characterizes him as a "facile sorcerer"; and later in the story Peregrine refers to him as a "failed magician." His career as a director has granted him a power over people that he has obviously enjoyed exercising, and the answer is "no" to the question he raises in the "Prehistory" section of the novel: "Have I abjured that magic, drowned my book? Forgiven my enemies? The surrender of power, the final change of magic into spirit? Time will show" (p. 39). Charles, who prefers to see real human beings as actors in a drama he is directing, revels in the "omnipotent imposition of form" that Murdoch distrusts, and he always opts for the "drama" and "magic" of an aesthetic approach to life, a choice that is apparent in his rationale for not marrying: "What suits me best is the drama of separation, of looking forward to assignations and rendezvous. I cannot prefer the awful eternal presence of marriage to the magic of meetings and partings. I do not even care for sharing a bed, and I rarely want to spend the whole night with a woman I have made love to. In the morning she looks to me like a whore" (p. 52). Charles prefers to see the women in his life as figures in paintings in the Wallace Collection, admitting that all women, with the exception of Hartley, seem shoddy in comparison with Shakespeare's heroines. He claims that he owes his entire life to Shakespeare and refutes Peregrine's accusation that he despises women in his assertion that he was in love with all of Shakespeare's heroines before he was twelve. Peregrine's reply, that these women do not exist but instead live only in the "never-never land of art, all tricked out in Shakespeare's wit and wisdom. . . . The real thing is spite and lies and arguments about money," is lost on Charles (p. 163). Characteristically, the comical short history of his love affair with Lizzie is chronologically summarized in theatrical terms:

> She fell in love with me during *Romeo and Juliet*, she revealed her love during *Twelfth Night*, we got to know each other during *A Midsummer Night's Dream*. Then, (but that was later) I began to love her during *The Tempest*, and (but that was later still) I left her during *Measure for Measure* (when Aloysius Bull was playing the Duke). (P. 49)

Characters in the novel are often described by Charles in terms of whatever role they have chosen to play at that moment, for his theatrical vision of the world often functions to obscure truth and reality and prevents an objective analysis of the people around him. Searching for the proper form his work should take, what he at first calls a "diary," a "memoir," and an "autobiography," he later joyously decides that it must be a novel—a movement from an ostensibly journalistic mode of expression to a fictional one that parallels his growing tendency, after his discovery of Hartley in Narrowdean, to dramatize and fictionalize what is going on around him. Shortly after announcing that he is actually writing a novel, he begins to construct an elaborate theory about Hartley's husband and their marital difficulties, a fact that leads James to attempt to convince Charles that he is fighting for a "phantom Helen" and to call his idea of rescuing Hartley from her husband "pure imagination, pure fiction" (p. 178); later he tells Charles that he has "made it into a story, and stories are false" (p. 335). During his last meeting with Charles he says that the pursuit of Hartley has been an emotional exorcism and that Hartley has been used as a kind of "image, a doll, a simulacrum"; as a result, he will eventually be able to forgive her. Earlier Charles has admitted that Hartley is an "image" he has created, but he denies that it is fictional: "It was only now clear to me how very much I had *made* that image, and yet I could not feel that it was anything like a fiction. It was more like a special sort of truth, almost a touchstone; as if a thought of mine could become a thing, and at the same time be truth" (p. 428). In a similar fashion Charles, who accepts responsibility for Titus's death, realizes that it was partially caused by his failure to warn him about the dangerous sea because of his egotism and pride in the boy's strength, but in this instance he admits that he preferred a fictional image to reality: "I did not want to spoil my picture of Titus or Titus's picture of me by any mean prudence" (p. 402).

Late in the novel Charles, now aware that his idealized portrait of Hartley is no longer possible, discusses how love can become an end in itself, self-perpetuating and independent of the love-object:

> But supposing it should turn out in the end that such a love should lose its object, *could* it, whatever happened, lose its object? . . . Would I at last absolutely lose Hartley because of a

> treachery or desertion on her part which should turn my love into hate? Could I begin to see her as cold, heartless, uncanny, a witch, a sorceress? I felt that this could never be, and I felt it as an achievement, almost as a mode of possession. As James said, "If even a dog's tooth is truly worshipped it glows with light." My love for Hartley was very nearly an end in itself. Twist and turn as she might, whatever happened she could not escape me now. (P. 430)

In *The Black Prince* Bradley Pearson acknowledges that although his novel was an attempted eternal embrace of Julian Baffin, this kind of artistic imprisonment is impossible because the reality of the individual will always elude the efforts of art or other human beings to fix him in a static position. Charles Arrowby, a much more egotistical, self-centered individual, denies Hartley this ability. In a sense his physical kidnaping of Hartley is merely a reflection of his need to hold her captive in his imagination, to create an aesthetic figure or image whose fate he can completely control, for he admits that he sees himself as a god-figure who must "create" Hartley's beauty: "I was all the time gazing with a kind of creative passion at her candle-lit face, like some god reassembling her beauty for my own purposes" (p. 221). Later, he tells Lizzie that he believes that he is able to "renew" Hartley as if he were God.

Wallace's belief that the unconscious self-exposure of the narrator is a comic device is relevant to the comic quality of *The Sea, The Sea*, in which the reader becomes gradually aware that Charles is erroneously interpreting events and conversations, blinded by his egotism and by the desire for his second encounter with Hartley to correspond to his romantic memories. The growing evidence of his irrationality and refusal to see the truth about their present relationship forces the reader to detach himself from Charles's consciousness in order to view the events of the novel from a more objective and critical perspective. Murdoch, who uses changes in narrative perspective to create comic effects in both *An Accidental Man* and *The Black Prince*, allows the discrepancy between Charles's and the reader's interpretation of events to create the humorous dimension of *The Sea, The Sea*. From the beginning Charles assumes that Hartley, still in love with him, regrets her refusal to marry him forty years earlier, and from this incorrect assumption follows all of the ridiculous and tragic events that he himself engineers. When Hartley comes to his home to tell the story of her marriage and to ask for help in finding her son, he refuses to listen to what she is really saying, instead interpreting her visit as an avowal of love and a desire to run off with him. His letters to Hartley, like those of Austin Gibson Grey, contain numerous lies about his past and present, and he erroneously and optimistically believes he will be able to "carry off" his old love. His statement in one letter that "I suspect, and forgive me for glancing at this, that you may have suffered more than one hour of remorse as you thought of me as living my 'exciting life' and how utterly, as it seemed, you had lost me" is extremely amusing in light of the fact that he has apparently forgotten that it was Hartley who rejected him (p. 205). The letter in which he claims that he will now begin to "tramp in and out" of her life is comic in its complete misreading of the reality of the situation he finds himself in, a situation made more humorous by the fact that Hartley leaves the letter behind unopened. Toward the end of the book his never-ending rationalizations for why Hartley has not yet "jumped down into his boat" are amusing and pitiful, and even after her move to Australia he looks for "hopeful signs" in the stone left in the garden and the unopened letter stuck in the linoleum. The reader, who realizes that all of this merely signals Hartley's indifference, just as her playing of "Greensleeves" on the recorder with her husband reveals how she has forgotten the past, is also aware during their last conversation that Hartley is shedding tears of pity, not sorrow—a fact that Charles fails to grasp.[14]

Charles's situation fails to be tragic because he too frequently reveals his basic contempt for Hartley, referring to her several times as a "beggar maid" who must be rescued by a "king," and clearly communicating his feeling of superiority to the woman he claims to adore: "She did not have to join my grand intimidating alien world. To wed his beggar maid the king would, and how gladly, become a beggar too. The vision of that healing humility would henceforth be my guide" (p. 373). His descriptions of her mustache, wrinkles, and aging body are similar to Bradley's descriptions of women in *The Black Prince*, for, although he makes an effort to conceal his contempt, it emerges in the physical picture he paints for the reader: his observation that Hartley snores and that Titus refuses to enter her room because of its foul odor are additional examples of his physical degradation of his lost love. Hartley is aware of Charles's disdain for her and correctly accuses him of supercilious curiousity, saying that "it's curiousity, like a tourist, you're visiting me, visiting my life and feeling superior" (p. 300). His continual reference to her as a "girl" is both denigrating and comic, as is his melodramatic vision of Hartley as suicidal and self-destructive; the reader suspects that Rosina's description of her as an ordinary older woman who simply wants to rest is closer to the truth. In the same way Hartley's invitation to Charles to come to tea and his final encounter with her and her husband are comic in their anticlimactic quality; Charles, expecting some sort of explosive event, gets only sandwiches and polite conversation while still desperately looking for signs that Hartley wishes to leave Ben, and he fails to realize that the married couple are trying to extricate themselves from him as politely and kindly as possible. In fact, his incorrect assumptions and misreadings of the reality around him cause him to misinterpret the marital argument he overhears as proof that Hartley is miserable and will therefore wish to leave her husband, just as he erroneously assumes that Ben attempted to kill him.

Charles unknowingly reveals to the reader aspects of his personality that he either tries to hide or has previously denied. His egotism is apparent in his physical descriptions of himself and in his remark that he, unlike Hartley, has "scarcely changed" in the forty years they have been apart. His statement about his former actress-mistresses, that "all the ladies went downhill after I left them, except Rosina" (p. 52), and his casual observation about Rosina that "of course when I left her she never went back to Peregrine" (p. 74), further reveal his conceit. He simultaneously claims to have little interest in sex and yet enjoys discussing his affairs with what he calls his "girls," stating that a "harem situation would suit me down to the ground" (p. 48). Although he has earlier denied Peregrine's accusation of a homosexual affair with producer Fritzie Eitel, he makes a coy reference to "all those years I was somewhere else with Clement and Rosina and Jeanne and Fritzie" (p. 428). One of the major comic discrepancies in the novel is the fact that although Charles perceives Ben as the cruel, tyrannical figure in the drama and casts himself in the role of Hartley's rescuer, it is he who kidnaps and imprisons her. Similarly, even though Charles claims to be giving a strictly factual account of what is transpiring, it is his interpretation of the facts that is suspect, for his misinterpretation of events and efforts to mislead the reader qualify the tragic implications of the novel and lessen the reader's sympathy for him. Charles does admit at one point that he has been "less than frank" in his diary, but later stresses the accuracy of his "novelistic memoir":

> This novelistic memoir, as it has now become, is however, as far as its facts are concerned (though, as James would say, what indeed are facts?) accurate and truthful. I have in particular, and this may be a professional attribute, an extremely good memory for dialogue, and I am sure that a tape-recording of my candlelit conversation with Hartley would differ but little from what I have transcribed. My account is curtailed, but omits nothing of substance and faithfully narrates the actual words spoken. (P. 239)

Despite this assurance of accuracy, however, the reader is suspicious of the version of the story he is presenting, and, as a result, sympathetic involvement often gives way to critical skepticism. Charles considers his readers, whom he sometimes addresses directly, as the audience he supposedly left behind when he abandoned the theater. His definition of the theater as "an attack on mankind carried on by magic," and of its function as being "to victimize an audience every night, to make them laugh and cry and suffer and miss their trains. Of course actors regard audiences as enemies, to be deceived, drugged, incarcerated, stupefied," has significant implications for his attitude toward his literary audience, for though he claims to be striving to present the events of the novel as truthfully as possible, his theory of art is based on a much different proposition (p. 33). He claims that the medium that the novelist uses is on the side of truth, but is later delighted by his discovery that language, like the theater, can deceive:

> It has only just now occurred to me that really I could write all sorts of fantastic nonsense about my life in these memoirs and everybody would believe it! Such is human credulity, the power of the printed word, and of any well-known "name" or "show business personality." Even if the readers claim that they "take it all with a grain of salt," they do not really. They yearn to believe, and they believe, because believing is easier than disbelieving, and because anything which is written down is likely to be "true in a way." (P. 76)

Charles's sudden revelation that he is writing a novel rather than a diary is related to his discovery that language can accomplish the same kind of deception and trickery that the theater provided him as a theatrical director. The role of the artist, in Charles's view, is to obscure and manipulate the truth rather than to use art to illuminate and reveal; he falls prey to what Murdoch calls the "temptation" of art, allowing his aesthetic vision to be a form of egotistical self-indulgence that imposes a false structure on the formlessness of reality.

Charles's egotism is reflected in his self-conscious and self-satisfied attitude toward his novel, an attitude that creates a smug tone which adds a further comic dimension to *The Sea, The Sea.* His frequent digressions on food and cooking are invariably humorous, as are his comments about the progress of the novel. He is almost childishly delighted with the beginning of what he calls at this point his "autobiography": "My paternal grandfather was a market gardener in Lincolnshire. (There, quite suddenly I have started to write my autobiography, and what a splendid opening sentence! I knew it would happen if I just waited)" (p. 22). Later, he comments on his developing style in a detached yet self-satisfied tone: "I have been rereading the opening pages of my autobiography! How full, for me at any rate, of frightful resonance those statements are which I have made, with such an odd and sudden air of authority, about my childhood" (pp. 26–27). Though he condemns his "little sketch" of James as "too short and 'smart,'" he admits he feels it is quite "stylish" and later confesses to being moved by his descriptions of James and Peregrine. The pleasure Charles takes in fictionalizing his life, in transforming the real people around him into stylish sketches, parallels his desire to cast real-life individuals into a drama he can both write and direct. Like Bradley Pearson, he finds verbalizing his experiences a way to control what is happening, and he believes that this process can dramatize and intensify experience:

> I have just written out my account of Lizzie's visit as a story and it has somehow excited and pleased me to put it down in this way. If one had time to write the whole of one's life thus bit by bit as a novel how rewarding this would be. The pleasant parts would be doubly pleasant, the funny parts funnier, and sin and grief would be softened by a light of philosophic consolation. (P. 99)

Murdoch, who believes that the function of art is to reveal reality rather than to console its creator or consumer, here presents Charles as attempting to use art and the creative process for solace rather than revelation.

In *The Sea, The Sea*, Charles Arrowby joins the ranks of several other men in her novels, among them Martin Lynch-Gibbon and Bradley Pearson, whose passions cause them to metamorphose into comically lovesick and deluded individuals. Murdoch, who frequently presents the experience of falling in love from a comic perspective, treats infatuation humorously because she believes it is all too frequently another manifestation of egotism and the solipsistic fantasies that egotism breeds. In *The Fire and the Sun* she discusses this aspect of romantic love:

> "Falling in love" . . . is for many people the most extraordinary and most revealing experience of their lives, whereby the centre of significance is suddenly ripped out of the self, and the dreamy ego is shocked into awareness of an entirely separate reality. Love in this form may be a somewhat ambiguous instructor. Plato has admitted that Eros is a bit of a sophist. The desire of the sturdy ego . . . to dominate and possess the beloved, rather than to serve and adore him, may be overwhelmingly strong. We want to de-realize the other, devour and absorb him, subject him to the mechanism of our fantasy. (P. 36)[15]

Gilbert describes romantic love as "slavery," as a "trap" that is best avoided, and Charles's problem is that his love for Hartley is the obsessive, self-centered, fantasy-ridden love that Murdoch perceives as antithetical to a free and objective apprehension of others. He correctly calls himself a "madman" and describes himself in much the same terms as did Bradley Pearson in *The Black Prince*, continually running about his home like a frenzied animal in a cage.

Later, he acknowledges the obsessive irrationality of his love for Hartley in a confession that is similar to Murdoch's description of falling in love:

> I was in a state which I well knew was close to a sort of madness, and yet I was not mad. Some kinds of obsession, of which being in love is one, paralyse the ordinary free-wheeling of the mind, its natural open interested curious mode of being, which is sometimes persuasively defined as rationality. I was sane enough to know that I was in a state of total obsession and that I *could only* think, over and over again, certain agonizing thoughts, *could only* run continually along the same rat-paths of fantasy and intent. (P. 391)

Although Charles lacks Bradley Pearson's talent for ironically objective self-analysis, like Austin Gibson Grey he is capable of a degree of insight into his own condition, a fact that increases the reader's often waning respect for him. As in *The Black Prince*, this kind of detached self-analysis is humorous, for the reader watches Charles achieve insights that he is unable to act upon.

Murdoch, particularly in *An Accidental Man* and *The Black Prince*, uses various devices to alter the reader's perspective of events in order to temper the seriousness of the subject matter. In *An Accidental Man* letters, notes, and conversational chapters serve this function, while in *The Black Prince* postscripts by other characters extend the fictional boundaries of the narrative. In *The Sea, The Sea* Murdoch allows her narrator to effect what could be called a comic revision of the novel in his postscript; the final section of the narrative endlessly qualifies and contradicts the story Charles has told in the novel proper, which ends on an extremely serious note of repentance and revelation. Charles appears to have arrived at an understanding and acceptance of what has happened, goes to sleep hearing the sound of singing, and finally sees the seals he has searched for throughout the story. Murdoch cannot bear, however, to end the narrative on this serious note. Always intent on forcing her fiction back to her conception of reality as "messy," continually expanding, and shapeless, she adds a postscript by the narrator, appropriately entitled "Life Goes On," which begins with Charles's suddenly mocking both the conclusion of the novel and the pretense of art that attempts to impose conclusions and final interpretations upon the fluidity of real life:

> That no doubt is how the story ought to end, with the seals and the stars, explanation, resignation, reconciliation, everything picked up into some radiant bland ambiguous higher significance, in calm of mind, all passion spent. However life, unlike art, has an irritating way of bumping and limping on, undoing conversions, casting doubt on solutions, and generally illustrating the impossibility of living happily or virtuously ever after; so I thought I might continue the tale a little longer in the form once again of a diary. . . . I felt too that I might take this opportunity to tie up a few loose ends, only of course loose ends can never be properly tied, one is always producing new ones. Time, like the sea, unties all knots. Judgments on people are never final, they emerge from summings up which at once suggest the need of a

> reconsideration. Human arrangements are nothing but loose ends and hazy reckoning, whatever art may otherwise pretend in order to console us. (P. 477)

Charles's decision to readopt the diary form for his narrative reveals that he is aware that he has been fictionalizing his story for aesthetic purposes that conflict with a truthful rendering of events, and, although he would appear to be aware of the important differences between life and art in this passage, his problem throughout the novel has been his incorrect assumption that the dramatic shape of the theater can be transferred to life. In an early section of *The Sea, The Sea* Charles, sounding a great deal like Iris Murdoch, discusses the fact that the power of the theater lies in its ability to present human life as existing only in the present, without the demands of the past and the future to lessen its dramatic impact:

> Drama must create a factitious spell-binding present moment and imprison the spectator in it. The theater apes the profound truth that we are extended beings who yet can only exist in the present. It is a factitious present because it lacks the free aura of personal reflection and contains its own secret limits and conclusions. Thus life is comic, but though it may be terrible it is not tragic: tragedy belongs to the cunning of the stage. (P. 36)

In his postscript Charles acknowledges that life, like the fiction that represents it, is subject to the demands of the past and future; life has no "conclusions" because all perceptions and interpretations are in a state of continual flux. His postscript, an attempt to bring the novel closer to a realistic presentation of events and human nature, is comic in its refusal to come to any kind of conclusion: "If this diary is 'waiting' for some final clarificatory statement which I am to make about Hartley, it may have to wait forever," announces Charles, who goes through a series of provisional explanations and conclusions about Hartley, James, Titus, and himself that he continues to revise (p. 490). At times he seems to have gained a degree of insight into himself and his actions. For example, his statement that "I have battered destructively and in vain upon the mystery of someone else's life and must cease at last" appears to be a valid summary of what has happened (p. 490), and his characterization of Hartley as a "phantom Helen" and admission that much of his folly was a result of a mistaken belief in that "stupid Gallicism," "*On n'aime qu'une fois, la première*," apparently reveals a new realization on his part (p. 492). Pages later, however, he once again takes issue with this interpretation, just as his opinions about James undergo several modifications. This continual alteration of the story places Charles in a somewhat ridiculous light, causing the reader to wonder if he is indeed becoming the "elderly party" that he denies he is, with a memory he describes as "tiny, limited, and fallible" (p. 492). It is certainly evident that he has not developed, to any significant degree, a lasting self-awareness and understanding of the experience he has gone through; for the most part it appears that he has merely exchanged his Martello tower and the sound of the sea for the towers of the Battersea Power Station and the "eternal drama" of the Thames. In this sense Charles is similar to many comic characters in modern literature, for Wallace believes that the failure to achieve any kind of final insight is an important characteristic of modern comic fiction. Earlier comic novels, particularly those of the nineteenth century, were narrated by a deluded *alazon* figure who developed into the knowledgeable *eiron* character; narrators of modern comic fiction, on the other hand, fail to become any wiser by the end of the story than they were in their youth, a fact that frustrates the reader, who expects some kind of growth or self-discovery from the comic hero or narrator. In fact, says Wallace, the falseness of a conventional expectation of this sort may be one theme of the modern comic novel.[16]

In the postscript Charles moves farther and farther from his enlightened state at the end of the novel. His belief that he came to the sea to repent of egotism was actually quite correct, for his sighting of the sea monster was a visual representation of the crippling jealousy that had haunted him throughout his life. The vision of the universe he sees early in the story, his chance to recognize his unimportance in an infinite and ever-expanding universe, corresponds to the narrative devices Murdoch uses in the fiction to widen the reader's perspective of events and to create a fictive world that, like life itself, is protean and relative:

> Stars behind stars and stars behind stars behind stars until there was nothing between them, nothing beyond them. . . . All was movement, all was change, and somehow this was visible and yet unimaginable. And I was no longer I but something pinned down as an atom, an atom of an atom, a necessary captive spectator, a tiny mirror into which it was all indifferently beamed, as it motionlessly seethed and boiled, gold behind gold behind gold. (P. 146)

This objectivity and lack of egocentriticy is short-lived, however, and Charles instead embarks upon a quest for a "phantom Helen," attempting to relive the past and, in the process, assuming complete control over the lives of others.

The postscript alters the reader's narrative perspective in several other ways. Just as the gossip of peripheral characters was used to present distorted and trivialized versions of events in *An Accidental Man*, in *The Sea, The Sea* Rosemary Ashe tells Charles that she heard that he had been "persecuted by some mad village woman" and that "a boy friend of Gilbert's had been drowned" in a comically absurd (and incorrect) description of the events of the novel (p. 481). *The Sea, The Sea* also contains hints of a "shadow novel," as did *An Accidental Man*, for Charles first tells the reader that his story will be about his dead mistress, actress Clement Makin, and at the end of the postscript is still wondering if he will ever find the time to write about her:

> Yes, I wonder if I shall ever write that book about Clement? It is as if this book has taken up forever the space which I might have given to her. How unjust this seems now. Clement was the reality of my life, its bread and its wine. She made me, she invented me, she created me, she was my university, my partner, my teacher, my mother, later my child, my soul's mate, my absolute mistress. She, and not Hartley, was the reason why I never married. She

> was certainly the reason why I did not seek and find Hartley at a time when it might have been quite easy to do so. (P. 484)

In this passage Charles contradicts much of the novel he has written, a fact that calls into question, once again, his version and interpretation of the story and suggests that an alternate novel of equal length could have been written about a completely different subject. Significantly, Charles chooses to write about a fantasy relationship rather than relating the real-life story of his love affair with Clement Makin.

The postscript frequently degenerates into a series of observations about Charles's current social life, a "chattering facade" which serves to place him in the context of the worldly, trivial milieu he had earlier hoped to abandon. In the final pages of the novel Murdoch further reduces the stature of her "failed Prospero," for Charles, awaiting the return of Fritzie Eitel and preparing for a lunch date with a sixteen-year-old girl who wants to have his illegitimate child, emerges in the postscript as a rapidly aging man with an incipient heart condition whose fame as a director is quickly disappearing. Although he has refused to "abjure magic," it has been taken away from him, and he is indeed playing the "celibate uncle-priest" role that James predicted. In *The Sea, The Sea* Murdoch turns the power figure that appeared in earlier novels—Mischa Fox, Palmer Anderson, Emma Sands, and Julius Irving—into a comic character; it is as if her humorous treatment of Charles Arrowby announces her belief in the final impossibility of one human being's controlling another. Frank Baldanza, who believes that Murdoch wishes to keep her power figures hidden from a too-close analysis by the reader, says that they are "for reasons of esthetic effectiveness" always kept "at a teasing distance . . . one never has an 'inner' view of their nature."[17] While this statement is applicable to the power characters who appear before *The Sea, The Sea*, her depiction of Charles Arrowby is Murdoch's attempt to enter the consciousness of this type of individual and to reveal him as comically trivial, sometimes pitiful, and ultimately powerless. Charles's egotism is paralleled by his indecision, and in the final analysis the "magician" who fails to transform his own life can only continue to ask questions. Just as Bradley Pearson revealed his uneasiness with his subject matter by placing words in quotation marks, Charles's writing style is characterized by a penchant for asking question after question. As could be expected, he generally fails to arrive at any answers, and the novel ends, appropriately enough, with a question that is left unanswered: "Upon the demon-ridden pilgrimage of human life, what next I wonder?" (p. 502). The man who believed himself to be a "god" or "king" who could change life into art through magic and trickery is comically revealed to be an ordinary and relatively powerless individual over whom the formlessness and unpredictability of "transcendent reality" have triumphed.

Afterword

Iris Murdoch's work, which presents a fluid, unpredictable, and contingent world, shares several characteristics with contemporary British fiction. The modern British comic novel frequently depicts an inverted, protean, and sometimes demonic universe in which the hero's major attributes include the flexibility to adapt to changing circumstances and an imaginative approach to reality that may cause him to treat life as art. This desire for imaginative control over his surroundings accounts for the fact that the comic hero, often an artist of some sort, narrates or is the central figure in a comic novel which is the result of his aesthetic need to manipulate reality. Like many of the individuals who appear in modern British fiction, Murdoch's characters are intent on personal survival and view their lives from an artistic perspective. Murdoch differs from many of the comic novelists, however, in that her attempts to fuse tragedy and comedy depend upon a comic treatment of realistic and tragic subject matter, and her critical and philosophical writings clearly reveal her belief in the aesthetic and moral validity of comedy, a conviction that is reflected in her fiction.

Murdoch began her career with a comic novel, *Under the Net*, and her second work, *The Flight from the Enchanter*, further demonstrated her ability to treat rather dark subject matter from a comic perspective. Though several of her novels, among them *The Sandcastle*, *The Unicorn*, and *The Time of the Angels*, cannot be described as particularly humorous, comedy has always been an important aspect of her fiction and has been of central importance in the novels of the past decade. After the publication of *The Nice and the Good* in 1968, she has increasingly emphasized the comic dimensions of her fictive world and has used various technical devices to create comic perspectives on events and characters that are often less than humorous. In her interview with Jack Biles, Murdoch has said that she prefers her later work and believes she is now a more self-confident artist who is no longer afraid of destroying the form of her novels by what she calls "rambling about," a phrase that can be interpreted to include the narrative experiments that result in the comic dimension of her fiction.

The three novels analyzed in this study exemplify Murdoch's talent for creating realistic situations and characters, injecting somber or tragic events, and then denying the reader the consolation of a tragic response. Frye's theory that comedy contains elements of both romance and irony is useful for an understanding of the basic structure of these novels, for Murdoch inverts the plot structures of typical and romantic comedy and makes frequent use of the characteristics of ironic comedy. In *An Accidental Man* she conveys her vision of a random, godless, and comic world ruled by contingency and change rather than human attempts at rational control, and she combines her ability to write the comedy of manners with the archetypal structures of Frye's scheme.

In *The Black Prince* and *The Sea, The Sea*, Murdoch uses first person narration as a comic device and continues to invert various types of comic structures. In *The Black Prince* she creates a novelist-narrator whose ironic perceptions of himself and those around him are responsible for the comic tone of the novel. Bradley Pearson, ironist and buffoon, prophet and fool, writes a novel that reflects in structure and tone his comic apprehension of the world. Just as *An Accidental Man* embodies Murdoch's belief in the relationship between comedy and contingency, *The Black Prince* is her exploration of the concept of irony and its potential as a comic device. In *The Sea, The Sea* Murdoch returns to the theme of the relationship of art to life, employing a narrator who mistakenly attempts to impose aesthetic structures upon the formlessness of reality. In this novel Murdoch approaches from a comic perspective types of events and characters she had earlier treated with complete seriousness: the power figure of several earlier novels and the *princesse lointaine* theme of *The Unicorn* become comic rather than tragic motifs. Throughout her career Iris Murdoch has been moving toward a comic vision of the world, and her fictive universe has increasingly mirrored her conviction that the comic mode is the most appropriate vehicle for the novel.

Notes

Preface

1. A. S. Byatt, *Degrees of Freedom: The Novels of Iris Murdoch* (New York: Barnes and Noble, Inc., 1965), p. 181; Richard B. Sale, "An Interview in New York with Walter Allen," *Studies in the Novel* 3 (1971): 424; Frederick Karl, *A Reader's Guide to the Contemporary English Novel*, rev. ed. (New York: The Noonday Press, 1972), p. 338.
2. Donna Gerstenberger, *Iris Murdoch* (Lewisburg, Pa.: Bucknell University Press, 1975), p. 15.
3. "Speaking of Writing: Iris Murdoch," *The Times*, 13 February 1964, p. 15, col. 2.
4. Ibid.
5. Ronald Bryden, "Living Dolls," review of *An Unofficial Rose*, by Iris Murdoch, *Spectator* 208, no. 8 (June 1962): 756.

Chapter 1: Introduction

1. Sigmund Freud, *Wit and its Relation to the Unconscious*, trans. A. A. Brill (London: Kegan Paul, Trench, Trubner, and Co., 1922), p. 336.
2. Aristotle, in his brief history of comedy in the *Poetics*, discusses how the writing of invectives by the "less dignified sort of writer" who imitated "inferior men" was one of the sources of comedy. *Aristotle's Poetics*, trans. Leon Golden (Englewood Cliffs, N.J.: Prentice-Hall, Inc., 1968), p. 8. O. B. Hardison, in his commentary, states that Aristotle believed that the true line of comedy was the "fictional comedy" of Middle and New Comedy, not the personal invective of Aristophanes. *Poetics*, trans. Leon Golden, p. 106.
3. In his definition of comedy Aristotle also stresses this painless aspect. He defines the "ridiculous," which is a characteristic of the baser men whom comedy imitates, as "some error or ugliness that is painless and has no harmful effects." *Poetics*, trans. Leon Golden, p. 9.
4. Sigmund Freud, "Humour," in *The Standard Edition of the Complete Psychological Works of Sigmund Freud: The Future of an Illusion, Civilization and its Discontents, and other Works*. Trans. and ed. James Strachey in collabora-

tion with Anna Freud (London: The Hogarth Press, and the Institute of Psycho-Analysis, 1961), p. 162.

5. Henri Bergson, "Laughter," in *Comedy*, ed. Wylie Sypher (New York: Doubleday and Company, Inc., 1956), p. 64. Freud's debt to Bergson is apparent here, for both discuss the need for an absence of feeling on the part of the laugher and the need for what Freud calls "psychic agreement" with the audience.

6. William McCollum's study of comedy, *The Divine Average* (Cleveland: The Press of Case Western Reserve University, 1971), defines comedy as an attempt to reinstate the norm that Bergson is speaking of here. However, unlike Bergson, he believes that it is the comic character who becomes "indistinguishable from the action of which he is a part, the theme or idea he embodies." *The Divine Average*, p. 95.

7. Yeats, in "The Tragic Theatre," in *Essays and Introductions* (New York: The MacMillan Company, 1968), pp. 238–45, presents an entirely different view of the comic character, saying that tragedy deals with universal types while "character is continuously present in comedy alone." "The Tragic Theatre," p. 240. Wylie Sypher, in "The Meanings of Comedy," in *Comedy*, ed. Wylie Sypher (New York: Doubleday and Co., 1956), pp. 193–258, quotes Mme. de Staël as echoing Yeats's belief that it is tragedy that "blurs the finer distinctions" between tragic characters, whereas comedy requires more knowledge of the human heart. "The Meanings of Comedy," p. 207.

8. Bergson, "Laughter," p. 148.

9. Ibid., pp. 170–71.

10. Ibid., pp. 148–49. Cf. Sypher, "The Meanings of Comedy," p. 206.

11. George Meredith, "An Essay on Comedy," in *Comedy*, ed. Wylie Sypher (New York: Doubleday and Co., Inc., 1956), p. 47.

12. Meredith, "An Essay on Comedy," pp. 43–44.

13. George Meredith, *The Egoist* (Boston: Houghton Mifflin Co., 1958), pp. 7–8.

14. Susanne K. Langer, "The Great Dramatic Forms: The Comic Rhythm," in *Feeling and Form* (New York: Charles Scribner's Sons, 1953), p. 333. Harold Watts's theory of the cyclical nature of comedy and of the linear nature of tragedy parallels Langer's distinction between comedy and tragedy. "Myth and Drama," in *Myth and Literature: Contemporary Theory and Practice*, ed. John B. Vickery (Lincoln: University of Nebraska Press, 1966), pp. 75–85.

15. Langer, "The Great Dramatic Forms," p. 331.

16. G. W. F. Hegel, *Lectures on the Philosophy of Fine Art*, cited in *Theories of Comedy*, ed. Paul Lauter (Garden City, N.Y.: Anchor Books, Doubleday and Co., Inc., 1964), p. 350.

17. Freud, *Wit and its Relation to the Unconscious*, p. 316.

18. Robert Bernard Martin, "Notes Toward a Comic Fiction," in *The Theory of the Novel: New Essays*, ed. John Halperin (New York: Oxford University Press, 1974), p. 72, agrees that comedy is an attitude of the mind that predates literary form.

19. Northrop Frye, *Anatomy of Criticism: Four Essays* (Princeton, N.J.: Princeton University Press, 1957), p. 171.

20. Bergson sidesteps investigating what he calls the "pessimistic" nature of comedy, in "Laughter," p. 188.

21. Morton Gurewitch, *Comedy: The Irrational Vision* (Ithaca, N.Y.: Cornell University Press, 1975); Walter Kerr, *Tragedy and Comedy* (New York: Simon and Schuster, 1967); Robert Heilman, *The Ways of the World: Comedy and Society* (Seattle: University of Washington Press, 1978).

22. Sypher, "The Meanings of Comedy," p. 242.

23. Compare Joseph Campbell, *The Hero with a Thousand Faces* (Princeton, N.J.: Princeton University Press, 1949), pp. 25–30.

24. Sypher, "The Meanings of Comedy," p. 206.

25. Gurewitch, *Comedy*, p. 48.

26. Ibid., pp. 84–85.

27. Heilman, *The Ways of the World*, p. 10.

28. Heilman's "group wisdom" corresponds to Meredith's "wiser world," and his theory of comedy contradicts Freud's belief that humor is a refusal to acknowledge the unpleasant aspects of reality.

29. Heilman, *The Ways of the World*, p. 231.

30. Kerr, *Tragedy and Comedy*, p. 16. Northrop Frye makes this point in his essay "The Argument of Comedy," in *Theories of Comedy*, ed. Paul Lauter (Garden City, N.Y.: Anchor Books, Doubleday and Co., Inc., 1964), p. 455, in his statement that "tragedy is really implicit or uncompleted comedy . . . comedy contains a potential tragedy within itself."

31. Kerr, *Tragedy and Comedy*, p. 199.

32. Enid Welsford, *The Fool, His Social and Literary History* (London, 1940; reprint ed. Gloucester, Mass.: Peter Smith, 1966), p. 313. Welsford describes at length the 1805 Christmas Pantomime, which featured the clown Joseph Grimaldi turning himself into a variety of objects and personalities, and discusses the transformation of "the little, every-day annoyances . . . into something strange and terrific." *The Fool*, p. 314.

33. Welsford, *The Fool*, pp. 201–2. Erich Segal, in *Roman Laughter* (Cambridge, Mass.: Harvard University Press, 1968), uses the principle of the Roman Saturnalia as a basis for his theory of Plautine comedy as a "holiday for the super-ego," a release from societal strictures.

34. Evelyn Waugh, *Decline and Fall* (Boston: Little, Brown, and Dell Publishing Co., 1948), p. 15.

35. John Wain, *Hurry on Down* (Harmondsworth, Middlesex, England: Penguin Books, Ltd., 1953), p. 35.

36. Welsford, *The Fool*, pp. 291–92.

37. Ronald Wallace, "Never Mind That the Nag's a Pile of Bones: The Modern Comic Novel and the Comic Tradition," *Texas Studies in Literature and Language* 19 (1977): 8.

38. Watts, "Myth and Drama," pp. 75–85.

39. Wain, *Hurry on Down*, p. 223.

40. Welsford, *The Fool*, p. 326.

41. In his study of the picaresque tradition Stuart Miller discusses this aspect of the picaro. He stresses his overwhelming desire to live and his ability to assume "protean forms," and believes that "There is no part he will not play." *The Picaresque Novel* (Cleveland: The Press of Case Western Reserve University, 1967), p. 70. However, Miller draws a distinction between the comic and picaresque genres, maintaining that comedy "celebrates the triumph of imagination over experience" while the picaresque novel reveals "the submission of the individual personality to chaos." Miller, *The Picaresque Novel*, p. 133.

42. Sypher, "The Meanings of Comedy," p. 232.

43. Waugh, *Decline and Fall*, p. 269.

44. Wallace makes this point in his article. The modern comic figure, unlike the hero of earlier comedy, does not attempt the integration of society. Rather, this new type of fiction focuses on escape through artistic creation. Comic protagonists try to create new worlds by fictionalizing their experiences; Wallace uses Humbert Humbert as an example. Wallace, "Never Mind That," p. 13.

45. Miller, *The Picaresque Novel*, pp. 65–66.

46. Iris Murdoch, *A Severed Head* (New York: Viking Press, 1961), p. 88.

47. Samuel Beckett, *Murphy* (New York: Grove Press, Inc., 1938), p. 111.

48. It seems equally true, however, that omniscient narration can serve opposite ends. The omniscient narrator can, through his limitless knowledge of human nature and events and his control of the narrative structure, create a sense of tragic inevitability.

49. Wallace, "Never Mind That," p. 17.

50. Watts, "Myth and Drama," p. 79.

Chapter 2: Iris Murdoch's Comic Fiction: Theory and Practice

1. Frederick Karl, *A Reader's Guide to the Contemporary English Novel*, rev. ed. (New York: The Noonday Press, 1972), p. 338.

2. June Sturrock, "Good and the Gods of *The Black Prince*," *Mosaic* 10, no. 2 (1977): 140.

3. Larry Jean Rockefeller, "Comedy and the Early Novels of Iris Murdoch," Ph.D. diss., Bowling Green State University 1968, p. 214. G. S. Fraser, in "Iris Murdoch: The Solidity of the Normal," says that Murdoch is not a "natural wit" and means this as praise, for, like Rockefeller, he has a basic distrust of comedy. Wit, he says, "can be a positive handicap to a novelist, lying like a kind of thin deadening glaze between the reader and the represented life or scene." In *International Literary Annual*, no. 2., ed. John Wain (London: John Calder, Ltd., 1959), p. 53. Malcolm Bradbury, in *Possibilities: Essays on the State of the Novel* (London: Oxford University Press,

1973), p. 31, takes an opposite view, stating that comedy and fiction have a natural affinity for one another: "There is a significant relationship between the novel form and the comic mode—a mode which, of course, transcends the novel, but seems to attach itself particularly closely to some of the novel's most familiar business." Walter Allen agrees that there is a close relationship between comedy and fiction: "It seems to me that the novel, simply because it is the novel, is bound to be comic. The novelist sets out to present a critical view of society. And as soon as you get a critical view of society, you get satire, a picture of the absurdities of those being criticized. So one can say that the comic is one of the permanent, surviving aspects of the novel, anyway." Richard B. Sale, "An Interview in New York with Walter Allen," *Studies in the Novel* 3 (1971):409.

4. Frank Baldanza, *Iris Murdoch* (New York: Twayne Publishers, 1974), p. 15.

5. A. S. Byatt, *Degrees of Freedom: The Novels of Iris Murdoch* (New York: Barnes and Noble, Inc., 1965), p. 211.

6. William Van O'Connor, *The New University Wits and the End of Modernism* (Carbondale, Ill.: Southern Illinois University Press, 1963), pp. 69–70.

7. Peter Wolfe, *The Disciplined Heart: Iris Murdoch and her Novels* (Columbia, Mo.: University of Missouri Press, 1966), p. 211.

8. William Hall, in "'The Third Way': The Novels of Iris Murdoch," *Dalhousie Review* 46 (1966):312, states that Murdoch's true talent as a comic writer lies not in the Rainborough-Agnes Casement relationship or the Artemis scene in *The Flight from Enchanter,* but rather in the "more consistent, quite unusual blend of the serious and the comic" in several scenes in *The Sandcastle.* Gerstenberger believes that the comic mode prevails in *Bruno's Dream,* a novel that comes close to a "successful joining of domestic comedy and macabre elements," *Iris Murdoch,* p. 49, and G. S. Fraser, in his discussion of *The Bell,* talks about Murdoch's use not of "riotous" humor but "a genial sense of the element of absurdity in all human conduct . . . even at the most tragic or intense or lyrical moments." "Iris Murdoch," *International Literary Annual,* p. 48.

9. Iris Murdoch, "The Sublime and the Good," *Chicago Review* 13, no. 3 (1959): 53.

10. W. K. Rose, "An Interview with Iris Murdoch," *Shenandoah* 19 (1968): 15.

11. Ibid., p. 22.

12. Ibid., p. 21.

13. Jack I. Biles, "Interview with Iris Murdoch," *Studies in the Literary Imagination* 11, no. 2 (1978): 117.

14. Michael Bellamy, "An Interview with Iris Murdoch," *Contemporary Literature* 18 (1977): 131–32.

15. Iris Murdoch, *The Sacred and Profane Love Machine* (New York: Viking Press, 1974), pp. 129–30.

16. Iris Murdoch, *A Word Child* (New York: Viking Press, 1975), p. 382.

17. Iris Murdoch, *The Sea, The Sea* (New York: Viking Press, 1978), p. 36.

18. Iris Murdoch, *The Fire and the Sun: Why Plato Banished the Artists* (Oxford: Oxford University Press, 1977), pp. 73–74.

19. Iris Murdoch, *Henry and Cato* (New York: Viking Press, 1976), pp. 158–59. In *Bruno's Dream*, the novel in which Murdoch's interest in Zen philosophy is most evident, she has the mysterious Nigel Boase instruct Diana Greensleave to allow those around her "to walk on her"; Montague Small in *The Sacred and Profane Love Machine* gives the same advice to Harriet Gavender. Murdoch's belief in what she calls "unselfing" and in allowing other people to exist independently is seen here, and it is apparent that she connects the ability to negate the self with the ability to view the world, and oneself, from a comic perspective. It is significant that Harriet, who dies a martyr's death protecting her husband's illegitimate son from terrorists' bullets, is treated comically to a degree throughout the novel.

20. Murdoch, *The Fire and the Sun*, p. 80.

21. Ibid., p. 84.

22. Iris Murdoch, *The Black Prince* (New York: Viking Press, 1973), p. 365.

23. Iris Murdoch, *The Sovereignty of Good over Other Concepts* (Cambridge: Cambridge University Press, 1967), p. 14.

24. Ibid., p. 15.

25. Iris Murdoch, "The Idea of Perfection," *Yale Review* 53 (1964): 379.

26. Iris Murdoch, "On 'God' and 'Good,'" in *The Sovereignty of Good* (London: Routledge and Kegan Paul, 1970), p. 54. Although early in her career Murdoch was fairly sympathetic with the existential position, she has become progressively more disenchanted with its philosophical tenets. Cyrena Norman Pondrum, in an article that focuses on *An Unofficial Rose* because she believes it is Murdoch's first clear rebuttal in fictional form to Sartrian ideas of freedom, has examined the differences between Murdoch's position and that of the French Existentialists. "Iris Murdoch: An Existentialist?" *Comparative Literature Studies* 5 (1968): 403–19.

27. Murdoch, "On 'God' and 'Good,'" p. 51.

28. Iris Murdoch, "Against Dryness: A Polemical Sketch," *Encounter* 16, no. 1 (1961): 20.

29. Iris Murdoch, *Sartre: Romantic Rationalist* (New Haven, Conn.: Yale University Press, 1953), pp. ix–x.

30. Kerr, *Tragedy and Comedy*, pp. 161–62.

31. Iris Murdoch, "Salvation by Words," *New York Times Review of Books*, 15 June 1972, p. 4.

32. Rose, "An Interview," p. 16.

33. Marjorie Ryan makes this point in "Iris Murdoch: *An Unofficial Rose*," review of *An Unofficial Rose*, by Iris Murdoch, *Critique: Studies in Modern Fiction* 5, no. 3 (1962): 117–21.

34. Ryan, "Iris Murdoch," p. 120.

35. Murdoch, *The Sacred and Profane Love Machine*, p. 347.

36. Baldanza, *Iris Murdoch*, p. 21.

37. Iris Murdoch, *A Fairly Honourable Defeat* (New York: Viking Press, 1970), p. 244.

38. Ibid., p. 401.

39. Murdoch, *A Severed Head*, p. 237.

40. In an article on *Bruno's Dream*, he says that "the changes take place abruptly, and without the kind of accompanying complications that the reader of realistic novels has come to expect. It is this formal acceptance of unlikely events and startling peripeties, shared by the novelist and her characters, that is the most probable cause of critical discontent. The sudden changes of bed and heart that intrigued and offended readers of *A Severed Head* receive the same apparently perfunctory treatment in *Bruno's Dream*. The absence in these and other of Iris Murdoch's recent novels of the sense of outrage consequent on peripety looks to some like a critical failure, willful or blind, to observe the necessary laws of cause and effect. But the peripeties are not peripeties at all, they are recognitions, and as such there is nothing perfunctory in their treatment. . . . The deft handling of *anagnorisis* is the characteristic narrative achievement of *Bruno's Dream*." P. W. Thomson, "Iris Murdoch's Honest Puppetry—The Characters of Bruno's Dream," *Critical Quarterly* 11 (1969): 280.

41. Iris Murdoch, *Bruno's Dream* (New York: Viking Press, 1969), p. 286.

42. Iris Murdoch, *The Flight from the Enchanter* (New York: Viking Press, 1956), p. 52.

43. Murdoch, *A Fairly Honourable Defeat*, p. 89.

44. Murdoch, *The Sacred and Profane Love Machine*, p. 30.

45. Murdoch, *A Word Child*, p. 18.

46. Iris Murdoch, *The Italian Girl* (New York: Viking Press, 1964), p. 22.

47. Bellamy, "An Interview," p. 138.

48. Frye, *Anatomy*, p. 165.

49. Iris Murdoch, *An Accidental Man* (New York: Viking Press, 1971), p. 400.

50. Iris Murdoch, *The Unicorn* (New York: Viking Press, 1963), p. 107.

51. Ibid., p. 227.

52. Steven Kellman, who has an excellent description of Murdoch's differing opinions on fantasy and imagination, says that "imagination, which respects the contingency of the world, is a reflexive, provisional faculty, whereas fantasy naively distorts reality by hypostatizing it in inflexible myths. Fantasy, rather than being an emancipator, is a servile attempt to flee messy ambiguities for a realm of complacent artifice. Imagination, by plunging us into the complex mire of human existence, is thereby an exercise in free will. . . ." In "Raising the Net: Iris Murdoch and the Tradition of the Self-Begetting Novel," *English Studies* 57 (1976): 49.

53. Howard German, "Allusions in the Early Novels of Iris Murdoch," *Modern Fiction Studies* 15 (1969): 361. Robert Hoskins, in "Iris Murdoch's

Midsummer Nightmare," *Twentieth Century Literature* 18 (1972): 191–98, does an interesting reading of *A Fairly Honourable Defeat* as a parodic inversion of *A Midsummer Night's Dream;* R. L. Widmann, in "Murdoch's *Under the Net:* Theory and Practice in Fiction," *Critique: Studies in Modern Fiction* 10, no. 1 (1967): 5–16, reads *Under the Net* as a parody of many different types of fictional forms.

54. Peter Wolfe can be excused for his incorrect statement in *The Disciplined Heart*, p. 64, that "the shifting-point-of-view technique seems to be a more congenial method and one more clearly in line with her central tenets," because his book was written before the appearance of the first person narratives of the seventies.

55. Iris Murdoch, *The Red and the Green* (New York: Viking Press, 1965), p. 205.

56. Murdoch, "Salvation by Words," p. 4.

57. Iris Murdoch, *Under the Net* (New York: Viking Press, Compass Books, 1954), p. 62.

58. Murdoch, *The Black Prince*, p. 58.

59. Murdoch, *The Fire and the Sun*, p. 87.

60. Iris Murdoch, *The Bell* (New York: Viking Press, 1958), pp. 203–4.

61. Heilman, *The Ways of the World*, p. 247.

Chapter 3: The Comedy of Contingency in An Accidental Man

1. Frank Kermode, "The House of Fiction: Interviews with Seven English Novelists," *Partisan Review* 30 (1963): 64.

2. Ronald Bryden, "Talking to Iris Murdoch," *The Listener*, 4 April 1968, p. 434.

3. Kermode, "House of Fiction," p. 63.

4. Rose, "An Interview," p. 11.

5. Bryden, "Talking to Iris Murdoch," p. 434.

6. Murdoch, "Against Dryness," p. 20.

7. Murdoch, "On 'God' and 'Good,'" p. 54.

8. Iris Murdoch, "The Sublime and the Beautiful Revisited," *Yale Review* 49 (1959): 260.

9. Murdoch, *The Sovereignty of Good over Other Concepts*, p. 32.

10. Ibid., pp. 3–4.

11. Murdoch, *An Accidental Man*, p. 433. Hereafter all page references to this book will be indicated parenthetically.

12. Though Garth is obviously speaking for Murdoch here, the more "decent" aspects of "hole and corner" acts are not emphasized in the novel. One of Garth's weaknesses is that he, unlike Jake Donaghue in *Under the Net*, fails to come to terms with contingency.

13. Baldanza, *Iris Murdoch*, p. 167.

14. Frye, *Anatomy*, p. 229.

15. Margaret Scanlon, "The Machinery of Pain: Romantic Suffering in Three Works of Iris Murdoch," *Renascence* 29 (1977): 71. Scanlon correctly observes that Patrick's insights are repeatedly dramatized throughout the novel.

16. Scanlon, "The Machinery of Pain," p. 77.

17. Baldanza, *Iris Murdoch*, p. 167.

18. This scene begins comically because the reader makes the assumption that Mavis and Austin are discussing Dorina's death; only as the scene progresses does it become obvious that Austin, in another display of obsessed egotism, is discussing his injured hand.

19. Langer, *Feeling and Form*, p. 331.

Chapter 4: The Artist as Eiron in The Black Prince

1. Wallace, p. 5.

2. Ibid., p. 19.

3. Francis M. Cornford, *The Origin of Attic Comedy* (London: Edward Arnold, 1914), p. 210. Cornford uses Aristotle's classification of the three major types of comic characters: the Buffoon (*bomolochos*), the Ironical type (*eiron*), and the Impostor (*alazon*), and states that the evidence for this is in *Tractatus Coislinianus*.

4. Cornford, *The Origin of Attic Comedy*, p. 137.

5. Sypher, "The Meanings of Comedy," pp. 229–33.

6. Murdoch, *The Black Prince*, p. 241. Hereafter all page references to this book will be indicated parenthetically.

7. Wallace, p. 16.

8. Cornford, *The Origin of Attic Comedy*, p. 154.

9. Ibid., p. 139.

10. Wallace, p. 13.

11. Ibid., p. 14.

12. Bradley Pearson's initials, which correspond to the title of the book, further reveal his identification with Hamlet. Hamlet is the "black prince" in *The Black Prince*, but the title has additional meanings. The black prince also refers to the "Black Eros" that Bradley mentions, the sexual and creative force that enables him to write his novel. Murdoch often uses symbols that, because they function ambiguously, are open to a number of different interpretations. In this work her title suggests Bradley, Hamlet, and a more obscure, almost godlike entity that affects Bradley throughout the narrative. Significantly, it is when Julian dresses as Hamlet that Bradley finally is able to make love to her, for it is at Patara that the three possible meanings of the title fuse.

13. Kennedy Fraser, "Ordinary Human Jumble," review of *The Black Prince*, by Iris Murdoch, *New Yorker* 49, 30 July 1973, p. 69.

14. Murdoch, *The Sacred and Profane Love Machine*, p. 33.

15. Sypher, "The Meanings of Comedy," p. 233.
16. Martin Price, "New Books in Review," review of *The Black Prince*, by Iris Murdoch, *Yale Review* 63 (1973): 81.
17. Sturrock, "Good and the Gods," p. 140.

Chapter 5: The Director as Alazon *in* The Sea, The Sea

1. Wallace, pp. 4–5.
2. Ibid., p. 14.
3. Frye, *Anatomy*, p. 183.
4. Ibid., p. 184.
5. Ibid., pp. 185–86.
6. Margaret Drabble, "Of Treacle Tarts and Eternal Love," review of *The Sea, The Sea*, by Iris Murdoch, *Saturday Review*, 6 January 1979, p. 53.
7. Murdoch, *The Sea, The Sea*, p. 210. Hereafter all page references to this book will be indicated parenthetically.
8. Frank Baldanza, "Iris Murdoch and the Theory of Personality," *Criticism* 7 (1965): 181.
9. Rose, "An Interview," p. 14.
10. Frye, *Anatomy*, p. 189.
11. Ibid., p. 195.
12. Biles, "Interview with Iris Murdoch," p. 117.
13. Bellamy, "An Interview," p. 135. Murdoch also discusses the temptation of form in "Against Dryness."
14. Murdoch, however, does leave Hartley's apparent forgetfulness open to a possibly different interpretation, for she does remember the mirror trick and the fact that James is Aunt Estelle's son. It is possible that Hartley is seeking revenge on Charles or is attempting to alienate him by pretending to have forgotten important aspects of their past relationship.
15. Murdoch, *The Fire and the Sun*, p. 36.
16. Wallace, "Never Mind That," p. 14.
17. Baldanza, *Iris Murdoch*, p. 19.

Bibliography

Primary Sources

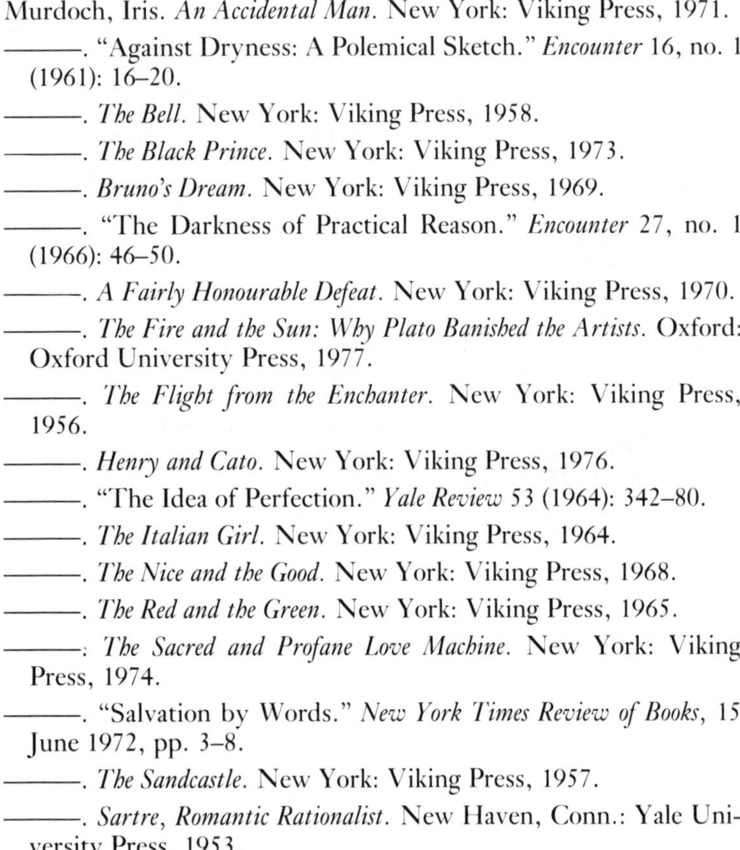

Murdoch, Iris. *An Accidental Man*. New York: Viking Press, 1971.

———. "Against Dryness: A Polemical Sketch." *Encounter* 16, no. 1 (1961): 16–20.

———. *The Bell*. New York: Viking Press, 1958.

———. *The Black Prince*. New York: Viking Press, 1973.

———. *Bruno's Dream*. New York: Viking Press, 1969.

———. "The Darkness of Practical Reason." *Encounter* 27, no. 1 (1966): 46–50.

———. *A Fairly Honourable Defeat*. New York: Viking Press, 1970.

———. *The Fire and the Sun: Why Plato Banished the Artists*. Oxford: Oxford University Press, 1977.

———. *The Flight from the Enchanter*. New York: Viking Press, 1956.

———. *Henry and Cato*. New York: Viking Press, 1976.

———. "The Idea of Perfection." *Yale Review* 53 (1964): 342–80.

———. *The Italian Girl*. New York: Viking Press, 1964.

———. *The Nice and the Good*. New York: Viking Press, 1968.

———. *The Red and the Green*. New York: Viking Press, 1965.

———. *The Sacred and Profane Love Machine*. New York: Viking Press, 1974.

———. "Salvation by Words." *New York Times Review of Books*, 15 June 1972, pp. 3–8.

———. *The Sandcastle*. New York: Viking Press, 1957.

———. *Sartre, Romantic Rationalist*. New Haven, Conn.: Yale University Press, 1953.

———. *The Sea, The Sea.* New York: Viking Press, 1978.

———. *A Severed Head.* New York: Viking Press, 1961.

———. *The Sovereignty of Good.* London: Routledge and Kegan Paul, 1970.

———. *The Sovereignty of Good over Other Concepts.* Cambridge: Cambridge University Press, 1967.

———. "The Sublime and the Beautiful Revisited." *Yale Review* 49 (1959): 247–51.

———. "The Sublime and the Good." *Chicago Review* 13, no. 3 (1959): 42–55.

———. *The Time of the Angels.* New York: Viking Press, 1966.

———. *Under the Net.* New York: Viking Press, Compass Books, 1964.

———. *The Unicorn.* New York: Viking Press, 1963.

———. *An Unofficial Rose.* New York: Viking Press, 1962.

———. *A Word Child.* New York: Viking Press, 1975.

Secondary Sources

Baldanza, Frank. *Iris Murdoch.* New York: Twayne Publishers, 1974.

———. "Iris Murdoch and the Theory of Personality." *Criticism* 7 (1965): 176–89.

Beckett, Samuel. *Murphy.* New York: Grove Press, Inc., 1938.

Bellamy, Michael. "An Interview with Iris Murdoch." *Contemporary Literature* 18 (1977): 129–40.

Bergson, Henri. "Laughter." In *Comedy*, edited by Wylie Sypher. New York: Doubleday and Company, Inc., 1956. Pp. 61–190.

Biles, Jack I. "Interview with Iris Murdoch." *Studies in the Literary Imagination* 11, no. 2 (1978): 115–25.

Bradbury, Malcolm. *Possibilities: Essays on the State of the Novel.* London: Oxford University Press, 1973.

Bryden, Ronald. "Living Dolls." Review of *An Unofficial Rose*, by Iris Murdoch. *Spectator* 208, 8 June 1962, pp. 755–56.

———. "Talking to Iris Murdoch." *The Listener* 79, no. 4 (April 1968): 433–34.

Byatt, A. S. *Degrees of Freedom: The Novels of Iris Murdoch.* New York: Barnes and Noble, Inc., 1965.

Campbell, Joseph. *The Hero with a Thousand Faces.* Princeton, N.J.: Princeton University Press, 1949.

Cornford, Francis M. *The Origin of Attic Comedy.* London: Edward Arnold, 1914.

Drabble, Margaret. "Of Treacle Tarts and Eternal Love." Review of *The Sea, The Sea*, by Iris Murdoch. *Saturday Review*, 6 January 1979, pp. 52–54.

Fraser, G. S. "Iris Murdoch: The Solidity of the Normal." In *International Literary Annual*, no. 2. Edited by John Wain. London: John Calder, Ltd., 1959. Pp. 37–54.

Fraser, Kennedy. "Ordinary Human Jumble." Review of *The Black Prince*, by Iris Murdoch. *New Yorker* 49, 30 July 1973, pp. 69–71.

Freud, Sigmund. "Humour." In *The Standard Edition of the Complete Psychological Works of Sigmund Freud: The Future of an Illusion, Civilization and its Discontents, and other Works*, translated and edited by James Strachey in collaboration with Anna Freud. London: The Hogarth Press, 1961. Pp. 161–66.

———. *Wit and its Relation to the Unconscious.* Translated by A. A. Brill. London: Kegan Paul, Trench, Trubner, and Co., 1922.

Frye, Northrop. *Anatomy of Criticism: Four Essays.* Princeton, N.J.: Princeton University Press, 1957.

———. "The Argument of Comedy." In *Theories of Comedy*, edited by Paul Lauter. Garden City: Anchor Books, Doubleday and Co., Inc., 1964.

German, Howard. "Allusions in the Early Novels of Iris Murdoch." *Modern Fiction Studies* 15 (1969): 361–77.

Gerstenberger, Donna. *Iris Murdoch.* Lewisburg, Pa.: Bucknell University Press, 1975.

Golden, Leon, trans. *Aristotle's Poetics.* Englewood Cliffs, N.J.: Prentice-Hall, Inc., 1968.

Gurewitch, Morton. *Comedy: The Irrational Vision.* Ithaca, N.Y.: Cornell University Press, 1975.

Hall, William F. "'The Third Way': The Novels of Iris Murdoch." *Dalhousie Review* 46 (1966): 306–18.

Hegel, G. W. F. *The Theory of Fine Art*. Quoted in *Theories of Comedy*, edited Paul Lauter. Garden City, N.Y.: Anchor Books, Doubleday and Co., Inc., 1964.

Heilman, Robert B. *The Ways of the World: Comedy and Society*. Seattle: University of Washington Press, 1978.

Hoskins, Robert. "Iris Murdoch's Midsummer Nightmare." *Twentieth Century Literature* 18 (1972): 191–98.

Karl, Frederick. *A Reader's Guide to the Contemporary English Novel*, rev. ed. New York: The Noonday Press, 1972.

Kellman, Steven G. "Raising the Net: Iris Murdoch and the Tradition of the Self-Begetting Novel." *English Studies* 57 (1976): 43–50.

Kermode, Frank. "House of Fiction: Interviews with Seven English Novelists." *Partison Review* 30 (1963): 62–82.

Kerr, Walter. *Tragedy and Comedy*. New York: Simon and Schuster, 1967.

Langer, Susanne. *Feeling and Form*. New York: Charles Scribner's Sons, 1953.

Lauter, Paul, ed. *Theories of Comedy*. Garden City, N.Y.: Anchor Books, Doubleday and Co., Inc., 1964.

McCollum, William G. *The Divine Average: A View of Comedy*. Cleveland, Ohio: The Press of Case Western Reserve University, 1971.

Martin, Robert Bernard. "Notes Toward a Comic Fiction." In *The Theory of the Novel: New Essays*. Edited by John Halperin. New York: Oxford University Press, 1974. Pp. 71–90.

Meredith, George. *The Egoist*. Boston: Houghton Mifflin Co., 1958.

———. "An Essay on Comedy." In *Comedy*, edited by Wylie Sypher. New York: Doubleday and Co., Inc., 1956. Pp. 3–57.

Miller, Stuart. *The Picaresque Novel*. Cleveland, Ohio: The Press of Case Western Reserve University, 1967.

O'Connor, William Van. "The Formal and the Contingent." In *The New University Wits and the End of Modernism*. Carbondale: Southern Illinois University Press, 1963.

Pondrom, Cyrena N. "Iris Murdoch: An Existentialist?" *Comparative Literature Studies* 5 (1968): 403–19.

Price, Martin. "New Books in Review." Review of *The Black Prince*, by Iris Murdoch. *Yale Review* 63 (1973): 80–83.

Rockefeller, Larry Jean. "Comedy and the Early Novels of Iris Murdoch." Ph.D. diss., Bowling Green State University, 1968.

Rose, W. K. "An Interview with Iris Murdoch." *Shenandoah* 19 (1968): 3–22.

Ryan, Marjorie. "Iris Murdoch: *An Unofficial Rose*." Review of *An Unofficial Rose*, by Iris Murdoch. *Critique: Studies in Modern Fiction* 5, no. 3 (1962–63): 117–21.

Sale, Richard B. "An Interview in New York with Walter Allen." *Studies in the Novel* 3 (1971): 405–29.

Scanlon, Margaret. "The Machinery of Pain: Romantic Suffering in Three Works of Iris Murdoch." *Renascence* 29 (1977): 69–85.

Segal, Erich. *Roman Laughter: The Comedy of Plautus*. Cambridge, Mass.: Harvard University Press, 1968.

"Speaking of Writing: Iris Murdoch." *The Times*, 13 February 1964, p. 15, cols. 2–3.

Sturrock, June. "Good and the Gods of *The Black Prince*." *Mosaic* 10, no. 2 (1977): 133–41.

Sypher, Wylie. "The Meanings of Comedy." In *Comedy*, edited by Wylie Sypher. New York: Doubleday and Co., 1965. Pp. 193–258.

Thomson, P. W. "Iris Murdoch's Honest Puppetry—The Characters of *Bruno's Dream*." *Critical Quarterly* 11 (1969): 277–83.

Wain, John. *Hurry on Down*. Harmondsworth, Middlesex, England: Penguin Books, Ltd., 1953.

Wallace, Ronald. "Never Mind That the Nag's a Pile of Bones: The Modern Comic Novel and the Comic Tradition." *Texas Studies in Literature and Language* 19 (1977): 1–23.

Watts, Harold H. "Myth and Drama." In *Myth and Literature: Contemporary Theory and Practice*, edited by John B. Vickery. Lincoln: University of Nebraska Press, 1966. Pp. 75–85.

Waugh, Evelyn. *A Handful of Dust and Decline and Fall*. New York: Dell Publishing Co., Inc., 1934.

Welsford, Enid. *The Fool: His Social and Literary History*. London, 1935; reprint ed. Gloucester, Mass.: Peter Smith, 1966.

Widmann, R. L. "Murdoch's *Under the Net:* Theory and Practice in Fiction." *Critique: Studies in Modern Fiction* 10, no. 1 (1967): 5–16.

Wolfe, Peter. *The Disciplined Heart: Iris Murdoch and Her Novels.* Columbia, Mo.: University of Missouri Press, 1966.

Yeats, William Butler. "The Tragic Theatre." In *Essays and Introductions.* New York: The Macmillan Co., 1968. Pp. 238–45.

Index